BERLITZ®

and Menorca

1991/1992 Edition

By the staff of Berlitz Guides

How to use our guide

- All the practical information, hints and tips that you will need before and during your trip start on page 101.

- For general background, see the sections The Islands and the People, p. 6, Facts and Figures, p. 11, and A Brief History, p. 12.

- All the sights to see are listed between pages 22 and 79. Our own choice of sights most highly recommended is pinpointed by the Berlitz traveller symbol.

- Sports, shopping, entertainment and festivals are described between pages 80 and 91, while information on restaurants and cuisine is to be found on pages 92 to 100.

- Finally, there is an index at the back of the book, pp. 126–128.

Found an error or an omission in this Berlitz Guide? Or a change or new feature we should know about? Our editor would be happy to hear from you, and a postcard would do. Be sure to include your name and address, since in appreciation for a useful suggestion, we'd like to send you a free travel guide. Write to: Berlitz Publishing Co., London Road, Wheatley, Oxford OX9 1YR, Great Britain.

Although we make every effort to ensure the accuracy of all the information in this book, changes occur incessantly. We cannot therefore take responsibility for facts, prices, addresses and circumstances in general that are constantly subject to alteration.

In this same series, Berlitz has published travel guides devoted entirely to Barcelona, the Costa Dorada and Ibiza and Formentera.

Text: Martin Gostelow
Staff Editor: Alice Taucher
Layout: Doris Haldemann
Photography: Ken Welsh; pp. 7, 20, 30, 56, 67 and 77 Martin Gostelow
We wish to thank Sarah Fleming, Anthea Inwoods, Martin Green and the Balearic Government Tourist Office for their help in the preparation of this guide.
Cartography: Falk-Verlag, Hamburg

Cover photo: Windmills on Mallorca's central plain Es Pla; *pp. 2–3:* Windsurfers near Fornells, Menorca.

Contents

The Islands and the People

Millions flock to Mallorca and Menorca from the colder north, and many return year after year, attracted by the reliable sunshine and warm, turquoise-blue sea; a choice package of flight, accommodation and meals; cheerful service by friendly people who understand what you say; plenty to do—or nothing to do; sensuous indolence or an adventure playground. And all brilliantly organized to keep the cost down.

There's always been a lot more to the Balearics, as the island group is called*, than beaches and bars, of course. And as activities augment or replace simple sunning, and the holiday season gets universally longer, the islands are attracting new admirers. Thousands of Europe's cyclists in rainbow gear take to the roads of Mallorca in March. April and May bring hikers to exclaim over the wildflowers. "Twitchers"—bird-spotters with binoculars and telephoto lenses—compete to record rarities and migrants on their way north. By June, human migra-tion in the opposite direction really starts to hot up. Many keep their boats here, anything from a dinghy to a millionaire's gin palace. This is a sailing paradise with safe harbours and marinas only a short cruise from quiet coves.

Those who have never been here claim that the islands are loud and covered in concrete: Mallorca has sometimes had a bad press; Menorca has had hardly any press at all. Believe the negative noises and you'll

---

* The other principal islands in the group are Ibiza and Formentera.

miss out on two treasure islands that can't be duplicated anywhere. Loud? In summer, certainly, in the brasher places, but it's the sound of people having the good time they came for, in the company they like. If you want to avoid the hubbub, and them, you can. Concrete? It's there, yes, but restricted to small areas. Climb to a hilltop and the resorts look like tiny white toytowns, mere pinpoints round the edge of undisturbed rural tranquillity.

When previous generations moved inland to get out of range of marauding pirates, it meant that today's islanders could live almost unmolested by the beach-bound majority of modern invaders. So, against the odds, much of the traditional life and values has been preserved. But repeated waves of

Holiday homes sprout in cactus garden at Cala Fornells on the north coast of Menorca.

visitors bent on pleasure inevitably had some effect on the local way of life. Farmland began to be left untended as people took jobs in the holiday industry or in constructing its facilities, although plenty of people still have "normal" occupations and keep a level head about tourism. Especially on Menorca, where cold winter winds limit the season's length. That prudence should prove useful for the health of the economy, now that the number of visitors is stabilizing after years of unstoppable growth.

The islanders have a well-deserved reputation for hard work. On building sites it often looks as if the labourers must be earning a bonus for every minute saved. Fishermen still put to sea in their double-ended boats, directly descended from Arab designs. If they need subsidies to make a living on today's diminished catches, so be it. Get off the tourist track and you'll find farmers cheerfully working lonely fields that look about as fertile as a main road. Their predecessors must have put the same sort of energy into shifting stone to build all the prehistoric villages, towers and monuments found on the islands: it largely explains how a small population could have achieved so much.

Land sales for development and income from the influx of visitors have made the Balearics the most prosperous region of Spain. You'll notice how some of the money has been spent putting houses into good shape; if you get a look inside them, you'll see the evidence of the population's love affair with consumer durables. The smallest village has its video rental "club", although there may be no other shops and nowhere to eat out. Nose-to-tail parked cars threaten to choke every street. And ubiquitous noisy mopeds symbolize the new independence of today's teenagers, who used to have a strict upbringing—especially the girls.

The locals stay amazingly good-natured in the face of the foreign flood, although their patience can get a bit frayed by the end of summer. It may be tested further as more outsiders buy into the old towns and villages, instead of being content with the holiday centres.

A quest for quality accommodation has led to more "country house" hotels in converted farms and mansions.

Folk costumes and crafts star at the La Granja country estate.

8

Summer crop of umbrellas mush-rooms at Cala Sant Vincenç.

Since these usually fill up as soon as they open their doors, further additions to the choice can be expected. Visitors are graduating, too, from sterile apartment blocks to houses and villas, to rent or buy or time-share. They're demanding more trees and green space around them and much more imaginative architecture.

Just in time (some would say late in the day), a powerful environmental conscience has found its voice. Campaigns have saved islands and bays as yet undeveloped. The regional government has imposed a tax on the building of leisure facil-ities, the proceeds to be used to buy land and keep it pristine. National parks and nature re-serves have been established. The goose that laid the golden egg of tourism is to be a protect-ed species.

Facts and Figures

Geography Mallorca and Menorca lie in the western Mediterranean, about 180 km. (110 mi.) off the south-east coast of Spain. They are the two largest of the Balearic Islands: Mallorca with an area of 3,640 sq. km. (1,405 sq. mi.) and Menorca 700 sq. km. (270 sq. mi.). North-western Mallorca is mountainous, with steep cliffs to the sea and few harbours. The south-east is hilly, the centre quite flat. Most of Menorca consists of gently rolling hills; the western end is flatter.

Population Mallorca 601,600; Menorca 66,900. Tourism greatly increases these figures in the summer months.

Major Towns *Mallorca:* Palma de Mallorca (Ciutat), pop. 320,000; Manacor, pop. 28,000; Inca, pop. 23,000.
Menorca: Mahón (Maó), pop. 23,000; Ciutadella, pop. 20,000.

Government Spain is a democracy and a constitutional monarchy. The king is head of state. Since 1983, many of the powers of the central government in Madrid have been devolved to 17 autonomous regions, one of which is the Balearic Islands, with its regional capital at Palma.

Economy Tourism has long since overtaken all other activities as the major earner. Farming remains important (fruit, vegetables, grain, wine and livestock) and so does fishing. Industries are on a small scale, and include leather goods, salt by evaporation of seawater, artificial pearls, textiles and ceramics.

Religion Predominantly Catholic (no longer the state religion), with small Protestant, Jewish and other minorities.

Languages Spanish (Castilian) is universally understood and used, especially in business communications and other dealings with the rest of Spain. But among themselves, local people mainly use their own dialects of the Catalan tongue, *Mallorquí* and *Menorquí*. Official and unofficial campaigns for bilingual signs, or signs only in *Mallorquí/Menorquí* (evoking a backlash in favour of Spanish), have resulted in a lot of repainting, sometimes in multiple layers. Wherever tourists go, their principal languages are widely understood, especially English and German. 11

A Brief History

People were living in the Balearics by about 5000 B.C.— that much the archaeologists tell us. We can only guess where they came from; the coast of mainland Spain is nearest, but still quite a voyage. At first they lived in caves and rock shelters, and hunted the only large animal on the islands, a species of small antelope now extinct. They raised domestic livestock from about 3000 B.C. and later turned to growing crops as well. In a landscape strewn with rocks and boulders it was natural to build simple stone houses and to clear fields by piling the stones into heaps and walls.

By about 1200 B.C. construction had become more ambitious. Great towers called *talaiots* were being built; you can still find dozens in Mallorca and hundreds in Menorca. Even experts disagree about their exact purpose. The small dark space inside would hardly have been appealing to live in: it could have been a burial chamber. They made good watchtowers, and some became strong points in later defensive walls. They've given their name to a period and culture, the Talaiotic.

Besides the towers, you can still see entire prehistoric villages of substantial houses, such as Capocorp Vell (see p. 55) and Ses Paisses (see p. 51) on Mallorca. And on Menorca there's a feast of ancient architecture: ceremonial halls with roofs of massive slabs supported by rough columns, and *navetas,* burial chambers like upturned boats made of stone. Most beautiful of all, and unique to Menorca, are the *taulas,* tall vertical stones, each supporting a horizontal slab in an elegant T-shape.

Another sort of skill with stones was the islanders' deadly use of the sling, and it was this that brought them onto the world stage and into written history. Indeed, the name Balearic may come from the Greek *ballein,* "to throw". The Carthaginians absorbed the islands into their trading empire and founded the main ports, but they had learned to respect the slingers, and recruited thousands into their armies. In 146 B.C., at the end of the long Punic Wars, the Romans defeated the Carthaginians but didn't immediately move to take over the Balearics. Possibly they were reluctant to face a hail of missiles. By 123 B.C., however, they had pacified most of

Spain and, convinced of the need to tidy up the map of the western Mediterranean, they sent out an invasion force. The Roman ships were protected by coverings of hide against the stones and lead shot of the slingers. It was a rerun of David versus Goliath, but this time Goliath won, and the islands became outposts of the Roman Empire. Once in possession, the Romans gave the islands their present names, *Balearis Major,* which has become Mallorca, and *Balearis Minor,* Menorca.

The people continued to live in their villages around the *talaiots,* and the influence of the Romans on building seems to have been small. You'll see some sites where the conquerors merely reinforced the prehistoric walls, though they did found Palmaria (Palma) and Pollentia (near present-day Alcúdia). By contrast, the Spanish mainland was one of Rome's most important provinces. In the fifth century, as the Empire crumbled, tribes the Romans called "barbarians" poured into Spain. Goths were followed by Vandals, in turn pursued by

Giant taula *at Trepucó stands sentinel-like by its companion* talaiot.

Visigoths, who established themselves more permanently. The Vandals crossed to North Africa and there became a sea-power to be reckoned with. They occupied the Balearics until defeated by a Byzantine expedition sent from Constantinople in 534.

The Tide of Islam

Ignited in the Arabian peninsula by the teachings of the Prophet Muhammad, the faith of Islam spread like wildfire, with its armies reaching the Atlantic coast of Morocco by the year 683. Converts in North Africa included the warlike, nomadic Berbers, or, as they became known, the Moors. (The word was derived from "Mauretania", the Roman name for present-day Morocco.) They were determined to carry their new religion into Europe, and in 711 a predominantly Moorish army under the Arab general Tarik landed near the peninsula known afterwards as the Rock of Tarik (*Gibel-Tarik*, or Gibraltar). Within seven years almost all of Spain was in Moorish hands.

The vast Muslim world, from Baghdad to the Pyrenees, soon broke into fragments, and the Spanish part became an independent caliphate, with its capital at Córdoba. Under tolerant rulers the city rapidly became one of Europe's greatest centres of scholarship and the arts. At first the caliphs were content to accept tribute from the Balearics, without imposing Islam, but by 848 disturbances in the islands moved them to use their newly expanded navy to bring the region into line.

By the 11th century, the caliphate in its turn had splintered into a mosaic of fractious statelets (26 at one count). During the confusion, Muslim governors, including those on the Balearics, ruled as independent monarchs until new waves of zealots came from Morocco to enforce greater unity in the face of Christian resurgence.

The Reconquest

The aim of the Crusades was not confined to regaining the Holy Land: even before Jerusalem was recovered in 1099, popes and preachers had been calling for the Muslims to be thrown out of Spain. There were countless setbacks, but Christian kings and warlords gradually succeeded in forging alliances that set them on the road to the Reconquest (*la Reconquista*). In all, after the recovery of Jerusalem, it would take four centuries of sieges and battles, treaties, betrayals and still more battles before the Moors were finally overcome.

Muslim ports and shipping—in Christian eyes nothing more than the trappings of pirates—counted as targets for crusading, and a raid on Mallorca in 1114 overran most of the island before the attackers were forced to withdraw. On September 10, 1229, the Christians returned, this time for good, when a Catalan army led by King Jaume I of Aragón came ashore near the present-day resort of Santa Ponça. His 16,000 men and 1,500 horses, though outnumbered, were battle-hardened from mainland wars. The defenders retreated inside the walls of Palma, but on the last day of 1229 the city fell to the Christians and pockets of resistance in the rest of the island were soon mopped up. Jaume I was an enlightened ruler who made use of the talents of the Moors who had converted to Christianity, as well as of the large Jewish and Genoese trading communities, and Mallorca prospered.

The Moors on Menorca, on the other hand, quickly agreed to pay an annual tribute to Aragón (4,500 bushels of wheat and 600 head of cattle) and were left in peace. That tranquillity lasted until 1287, when the weak Alfonso III of Aragón, smarting over a series of humiliations at the hands of his nobles, found a pretext for invasion. The Moors were defeated and expelled or killed, leaving Menorca's economy devastated for decades.

Jaume I died after reigning in Aragón for 63 years, but he made the cardinal error of dividing between his sons the lands he had fought for so long to unite. At first this created a separate kingdom of Mallorca, under Jaume II, followed by Sanç and Jaume III. But inevitable family rivalry resulted in the overthrow of Jaume III by his cousin Pedro IV, who grabbed the Balearics for Aragón. Attempting a comeback, Jaume was killed in battle near Llucmajor in 1349.

Progress towards a single, Christian Spain continued through conquest, alliances and strategic marriages until only the kingdoms of Castile and Aragón remained. When their two heirs Ferdinand and Isabella, later to become the renowned "Catholic Monarchs", were married in 1469, the stage was set for the final act of the Reconquest. First Isabella ascended the throne of Castile, then Ferdinand that of Aragón. Isabella was the stronger character, who was to stamp on the dual realm a Castilian supremacy which persisted for centuries. (Some non-Castilians complain that it still does.) At last, a combined army marched against the only Moorish enclave left on the Iberian peninsula, Granada, taking it in 1492. For the first time in history, Spain was united.

World Power

As one age ended, another began. Even before the final defeat of Granada, Isabella and Ferdinand had received Christopher Columbus in the southern town of Santa Fe, which Isabella had ordered built for the purpose of conducting the siege. The captain from Genoa

(at least three Mallorcan towns dispute that he was a Genoese and claim him as their own) believed he could reach the East Indies by sailing west. In the same year that Granada fell, he crossed the Atlantic, landing in the Caribbean islands.

His feat marked the beginning of a century in which Spain exported its adventurers, traders and priests, and its language, culture and religion, to the New World, building a vast empire. Ruthless *conquistadores* sent back incalculable riches of silver and gold, arousing the envy and malice of other European powers, and Spain used her new wealth to exert influence and finance wars. The century and a half after 1492 has been called Spain's "Golden Age". In a literal sense it may have been that—in the arts it certainly was—but the era carried the seeds of its own decline. Drained of manpower and ships by such adventurism as the dispatch of the ill-fated Armada against England in 1588, plagued by corruption and incompetence, Spain became ineffectual at defending her interests. The Mediterranean was neglected, and the Balearics' promising commerce was attacked by Muslim pirates based in North Africa. The islands' coastal towns were continually raided and sacked by these "corsairs" and by the powerful Turkish fleet, despite rebuilding fortifications and constructing new ones inland.

Standing guard over Palma for seven centuries: the circular keep and tower of Bellver castle. **17**

French and British Ties

The daughter of Ferdinand and Isabella had married the son and heir of the Holy Roman Emperor, Maximilian of Hapsburg. The Spanish crown duly passed to the Hapsburgs, but they were sometimes more concerned with their other lands in Europe. Spain remained in their hands until the feeble-minded Carlos II died in 1700 leaving no heir. France, whose interests had perennially clashed with Spain's, seized the chance to install the young grandson of Louis XIV on the throne in Madrid.

A rival Hapsburg claimant was supported by Austria and by Britain, too, not out of any love for the dynasty but because a close Spanish-French alliance would be too powerful. In the War of the Spanish Succession (1702–13), which followed, most of the old kingdom of Aragón, including the Balearics, backed the Hapsburgs. Britain seized Gibraltar—in the name of the Hapsburg claimant, it might be noted—and retained it even when the war was over. In 1708 Britain also took Menorca, to get hold of the magnificent harbour of Mahón (Maó) for the Royal Navy; she hung on to it even when Bourbon forces captured Mallorca at the end of the war.

Menorca changed hands between Britain, France and Spain five more times in less than a hundred years. The French grabbed it first, at the start of the Seven Years' War in 1756; the Treaty of Paris returned it to Britain in 1763. A French-Spanish force landed in 1781 and bottled up the British defenders in an eight-month siege until the ragged remnants surrendered. By 1798, the British were back but finally gave up the island amicably to Spain in 1802, under the terms of the Treaty of Amiens.

By 1805, Spain was again aligned with France, and Spanish ships fought alongside the French against Nelson at Trafalgar. But Napoleon came to distrust his Spanish ally and forcibly replaced the king of Spain by his own brother, Joseph Bonaparte. A French army marched in to subdue the country. The Spaniards resisted and, aided by British troops commanded by the Duke of Wellington, drove the French out. What is known to British historians as the Peninsular War (1808–14) is called in Spain the War of Independence, and Spain's first constitution was drafted at this time.

Hopes of a constitutional monarchy were soon dashed, however, and the 19th century saw a succession of uprisings in the restless regions, often in the name of parliamentary democracy. The crushing of short-term republics by military coups, and Wars over the royal succession, left a legacy of hatred. Almost all of Spain's possessions in the Americas broke away in the wake of the Napoleonic Wars, and the few that were left were lost at the end of the 19th century. The beginning of the 20th—which saw the young King Alfonso XIII coming of age in 1902—was marked only by more crises, assassinations and near anarchy. Colonial war in Morocco provided an almost welcome distraction, but a disastrous defeat there in 1921 led to a coup in which the general Primo de Rivera became dictator. He was able to do the sorts of things that dictators do well—enforce public order, initiate public works—but he could only screw down the lid on the pressure cooker. He fell in 1929, and when the elections of 1931 revealed massive anti-royalist feeling in the cities, the king followed him into exile.

The Republic and Civil War

The new republic was born in an orgy of strikes, church-burning and uprisings of the right and left. Elections gave first the left, then the right, a majority. But parliamentary government never had a chance. The essential ingredient of compromise was totally absent. New elections in February 1936 gave the left-wing Popular Front the majority of seats in the *Cortes,* but in the country at large new extremes of violence took the place of argument.

In July 1936, most of the army, led by General Francisco Franco and supported by monarchists, conservatives, the clergy and the right-wing Falange, rose against the Madrid government. Ranged on the government's side were republicans, liberals, socialists, communists and anarchists. The ensuing Civil War was fought with such savagery and bitterness that even in a century punctuated by horrors it still stands as a landmark. Support for both sides came from outside Spain. Many people, often unaware of the particularly Spanish origins of the struggle, saw it as a crucial contest between democracy and dictatorship, or, from the other side, between order and Red chaos. The war lasted three years; the dead were uncounted but estimates range up to one million.

At the start, Menorca declared for the republic, and **19**

To small-scale farmers, traditional ways of ploughing are best.

stayed with it to the bitter end. Mallorca was seized by its garrison for the Nationalists, as Franco's forces became known. Early in the war, the republicans used their one battleship to support an invasion of Mallorca, but it ended in failure. One decisive factor was the presence at Palma of Italian air squadrons, used to bomb republican Barcelona. (Fascist Italy and Nazi Germany backed Franco's Nationalists; the Soviet Union supported the government, though less effectively towards the end.)

New Horizons

Exhausted, Spain was able to stay on the sidelines during World War II and began to make a recovery under the continuing tough law-and-order regime of Franco. There

foreign influences into Franco's once-hermetically sealed Spain.

Franco named as his successor the grandson of Alfonso XIII, who was enthroned as King Juan Carlos I when the old dictator died in 1975. There were dire predictions of a short reign, of violence, even of a renewal of civil war. But in complete contrast to most of his forebears, the king proved to have a genius for reconciliation and common sense. To the dismay of Franco diehards, he managed brilliantly the transition to democracy, and then stood back to allow it full rein. After years of repression, a great measure of autonomy was granted to Spain's regions, including the Balearics, and their languages and cultures enjoyed a renaissance.

More completely a part of Europe than ever before, Spain joined the European Community in 1986, giving a further boost to her booming economy. The new dawn brought a realization that unrestricted growth of mass tourism entailed damaging consequences: there came a new emphasis on quality and, especially in the Balearics, on safeguarding the environment. That, after all, was largely why people had wanted to visit in the first place.

had been a foretaste of foreign tourism in the 1920s, though of a rather exclusive variety. The tourist trade that began in the '50s and soon exploded into an annual rush by millions of sun-seekers was a new phenomenon, with a profound impact on the economy and the people. One effect was a rash of building on the coastline, at first with scant regard for tradition or aesthetics. Less visible, but perhaps more significant, was the influx of

21

Where to Go

Whether you're based in Palma, a coastal resort or an inland village, you can reach any point on Mallorca in half a day, and Menorca is even more concentrated. Newcomers are surprised by how much there is to do on what they may have thought were dots on the map. Tour companies offer excursions by road or in clever combinations with a boat trip, taking in the mountain and coastal scenery of the northwest, the beaches almost everywhere else, spectacular caves near the east coast, and various purpose-built attractions. These sights are rightfully famous, but inevitably they're quite commercial and you'll be part of a crowd, especially in high season. If you're offered very low-cost "tours", they are likely to be smooth operations to sell some product or other to a captive audience.

Hiring a car (see p. 107) lets you roam where you like, when you like, making your own discoveries. Some of the least-known places are the most delightful, so the further from the major roads you go, the more charmed you'll be. If you don't want to drive, use the buses—they go almost everywhere. Or rent a bicycle. When it's hot,

think about travelling in the early morning or making use of the long evenings.

We start in and around Palma, then make the tour of Mallorca in a clockwise direction, taking in all the highlights and plenty of diversions before finishing up in the centre. You can join in at any stage, and then conveniently head back to where you're staying when you have had enough sightseeing. Menorca rates its own section (see pp. 60–79).

We don't try to mention every beach or every village: it would take a lifetime of holidays to see them all. You'd still need several visits to cover the selection described here.

Palma de Mallorca
(Ciutat)

The Balearic capital's name in *Mallorquí* signifies simply "city", which hints at its importance in the minds of the islanders. Almost two-thirds of the permanent population of Mallorca live in Palma, and a glance at the map shows how the island's road system radiates from the city like the ribs of a fan.

Palm-fringed harbour handsomely sets off Palma's massive cathedral.

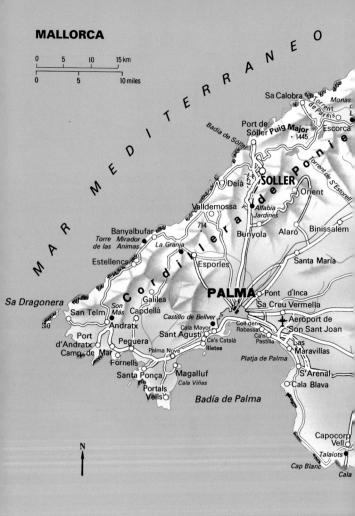

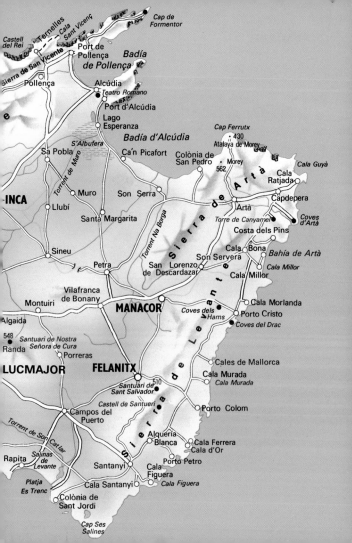

The romantic way to arrive would be from the sea at dawn or sunset. If you can't contrive to sail in on a sleek car ferry or a yacht, at least try to take a boat trip in the bay to see Palma from its best angle. Dominating the centre is the great Gothic cathedral, with the ancient Almudaina Palace beneath. To the east is Platja de Palma, a long line of sandy beaches stretching through Ca'n Pastilla to S'Arenal; to the west, the elegant promenade of modern Palma where luxury hotels look out over a forest of masts in the yacht harbour. Crowning the wooded slopes above are the white towers of Bellver Castle.

Ashore, there's plenty to see, starting with the old part of the city (*Centre Historic* on direction signs). On the waterfront, fishermen who still sail from Palma lay out their nets for mending. Palm trees drop dates on the bayside boulevard—it's something of a racetrack for competitive local drivers. Parts of the old city walls facing the sea still stand, though the rest were long ago levelled into a zigzag girdle of avenues.

Net-mending is a never-ending task for the Balearics' fishermen.

Below the walls, the **Parc de la Mar** is too unshaded and bare to please local strollers, despite its lake and a tile panel by Catalan artist Joan Miró. They prefer the gardens of **S'Hort del Rei**, next to the Almudaina Palace, though it's a matter of debate whether Alexander Calder's mobile *Nancy* belongs here. Most of all, they like **Es Born**, the elongated plaza that runs inland, for their early evening promenade. The line of the moat of the Arab city, it was later the site of jousting tournaments. Now, it's lined with cafés and park benches where businessmen meet over coffee and tourists rest their feet.

At the top of Es Born, **Avinguda del Rei Jaume III** imitates the architecture of a century ago, although it's actually much more recent. Expensive shops symbolize the sophistication of a city made rich by the tourist trade.

The **Palau Almudaina** was once the palace of the Moorish rulers. After the Reconquest it was remodelled for use by the kings of Mallorca. Part of it is open to visitors, and a short tour takes in the superb stone-vaulted 13th-century throne room, divided into two storeys in the 16th century—you'll see the window cut off in the process. In the heavily restored royal offices, used by the present king and queen when they're in town, traces of early paintwork survive on ceilings and frescoed walls. Down in the palace courtyard, dominated by the west front of the cathedral, the royal chapel of Santa Ana has a rare Romanesque doorway from the 14th century.

The massive Gothic **cathedral** *(La Seu)* was begun in 1230, immediately after the Christians recaptured the island from the Moors, and stands on the site of the former main mosque. Building was slow and sporadic, affected by wars and finance, and it was 1601 before the great work could be declared completed. Closely packed buttresses facing seaward create an extraordinary effect of power—and beauty, too, when they blaze like gold in the setting sun. They had defensive value: there was always the threat of bombardment from the bay. Walk round to that side to see the remarkable *Mirador* entrance.

The north door, near the 13th-century bell tower, is only open in the early morning and early evening. At other times, you have to go in through the nearby **Cathedral Museum,** a treasure-store of old manuscripts, relics of saints and portable altars. A colossal carved stone Renaissance doorway leads to the oval New Chapter House.

In the spacious cathedral itself, just 14 unusually slim columns support a soaring roof. The windows are fewer and smaller than north Europeans may be used to; in general, most Mallorcan churches are somewhat dark and fortresslike. But when the sun shines, the stained glass, some pictorial, most gaudy and geometric, lets in brilliant rainbows of light. The Catalan architect Antoni Gaudí added the Crown of Thorns canopy over the high altar at the beginning of the 20th century.

The **Palau Episcopal,** on a quiet square at the east end of the cathedral, houses the Diocesan Museum, with a diverse collection accumulated by archbishops over the years. In the narrow streets behind the cathedral, houses are so tall that they almost seem to meet overhead. Some are baronial **mansions** from the 15th and 16th centuries, with dark walls and great wooden doors. They may look forbidding, but try to get a glimpse through the heavy metal grilles into some of the courtyards. The **Casa Oleo** in Carrer Almudaina retains its Gothic architecture; even older

is the Arab **Almudaina Arch** which crosses the same street. Many courtyards were remodelled in 18th-century elegance. You'll see one at **Casa Oleza** (in Carrer Morey), a vision of wide-arched, cool patios, balconies and stately staircases.

Nearby in Carrer de la Portella a palatial mansion has been restored as the **Museu de Mallorca**. The collections are still being organized and labelling is only in Spanish, but relics of the Muslim period and fine 13th- to 15th-century paintings and carvings from Palma's churches make it worth a visit. The top floor houses exhibitions by present-day Mallorcan artists. Old photographs show some of the Arab gateways destroyed when the city walls were razed in 1902. Behind the museum in Carrer Serra, the **Arab Baths** *(Banys Arabs)* miraculously still stand after a thousand years, set in a garden decorated with ancient columns. The

horseshoe arches of the domed bathhouse are supported by capitals in various styles, no doubt gathered from earlier buildings. As in the Roman manner, the steam room had underfloor heating, and the adjoining vaulted room would have been the cooling-off area.

In Carrer Zavella the **Palau Vivot** is one of Palma's finest mansions. For years it was open to the public, but the pressure of numbers grew so great that the Vivot family had to call a halt.

Now you can only look through barred gates into the imposing courtyard. A few steps away, on the Plaça Sant Francesc, the **Convent de Sant Francesc**  (Convent of St. Francis) is one of Palma's treasures. In front stands a statue of Junípero Serra, 18th-century founder of the first missions in California, shown with a youthful convert. Inside the church lies the sarcophagus of the 13th-century sage and teacher Ramón Llull, along with Serra one of Mallorca's greatest sons and heroes—they have both been beatified, and sainthood seems sure to follow. An effigy of Llull lying on his side is perched high up in a chapel behind the altar, with delicately carved 14th-century stone niches below. Be sure to walk through to the enchanting cloisters: their slender double columns and stone tracery date from the same time. On school-days you'll hear children at work in the rooms above, and see paper aeroplanes in the cloister garden. Evidently they're not all aspiring saints.

You may have noticed another statue of Llull, bearded

Cloistered tranquillity reigns in the Convent de Sant Francesc. **31** and robed, near the Almudaina Palace. Just to the west, two Palma landmarks stand side by side. The turreted **Sa Llotja** was built in the 15th century by local architect Guillermo Sagrera (the seafront promenade here is named after him). Once the city merchants' exchange, and now used for exhibitions, it is one of Spain's finest secular Gothic buildings. Look inside if you can, to see its slim columns twisting their way through light and airy space to the vaulted roof. Next to Sa Llotja, cannons and an anchor surround the 17th-century **Consolat del Mar,** which used to be the maritime law court. Now it serves as the seat of the Balearic Islands' autonomous government.

The old city is full of pleasant surprises (but local people will warn you to avoid unpleasant ones by not carrying valuables that could be snatched in summer crowds). Walking is the way to see them best—distances are quite small and many streets are reserved for pedestrians. If you'd like to treat yourself to a tour in one of the horsedrawn open carriages, try to choose a Sunday when other traffic is light.

The **Plaça Cort** is the site of the wooden-eaved 17th-century Ajuntament (Town Hall) and from there it's a short way by smart shopping streets to the **Plaça Major**, the former marketplace. It has been restored and paved with glossy marble, though this has unfortunately not yet brought it back to respectability after dark. Today's market is under cover at the **Mercat** in Plaça Olivar, where you can marvel at the variety of consumables, especially fruit and seafood, and at the tumult of competing vendors and complaining housewives.

On Saturday mornings you'll see crowds flocking to the **Baratillo,** or Flea Market (even the signs on city buses call it by its English name). It's moved from place to place over the years and now occupies a big area of the Poligon de Llevante quarter east of the old city. You'll find everything from fans to fossils, including Mallorca's artificial pearls and lace—at "liquidation" prices, say the sellers, many of whom are gypsies or itinerant Africans. Don't miss the junk stalls, although it's hard to detect the boundary between items for sale and rubbish that happens to have been dropped next to them. Beware of the tricksters with three hollowed-out half-potatoes, who tempt you to bet on which one conceals a bead. You see some apparently easy winners? They're probably accomplices. In the vicinity, the **Museu Krekovic** houses strikingly gaudy images of Inca and Spanish history, products of the overheated imagination of a Yugoslav-born painter who lived in Peru and Mallorca.

When the evening promenade disperses, the streets of the old city are usually quiet, dark and almost deserted. There is more action if you head west. First to **Es Jonquet**, once the fishermen's quarter, now full of bars, cafés and clubs clustering under the old windmills which used to grind the city's flour. Along the seafront, the **Auditorium** furnishes a panoply of entertainment from opera to heavy metal. Further on, five-star hotels stand between the sea and the suburb **El Terreno**, where Avinguda Joan Miró and the Plaça Gomila ("Plaza Gorilla" to foreign jokers) are lined with cafés, discos and topless bars. Once the centre of Palma nightlife, the area is struggling to keep from being third-rate.

By day, take a tour of Spain without leaving Palma. A few hundred metres inland from Es Jonquet, the **Poble Espanyol** is a brilliantly designed walled town of replicas (some have had to be scaled down) of Spanish architectural treasures, from Toledo, Seville, Córdoba, the Alhambra of Granada and many other places. It's a multi-level maze which fits and flows so cleverly that there are no dead ends—even when you climb stairs. These are no mere façades, but real buildings housing shops, craft studios, bars and cafés. The sheer numbers of people going through have given it all the patina of age. Across the street, the same sort of inspiration has created a Convention Centre in the form of a Roman forum and theatre. Who knows what future archaeologists will make of all this!

You won't have missed the fine sight of **Bellver Castle** (*Castell de Bellver*), on its hilltop above modern Palma among pine trees and parkland. A magnificent piece of military architecture, it has commanded the sea and land approaches to the city since it was built in the 14th century by order of King Jaume II. The view from the circular battlements is stunning, and you'll see how the sloping roof funnelled rainwater into the castle's cisterns. Inside, there's a small, well-laid-out museum of the archaeology of the area. When you're hungry, head for the hillside village of Genova and its choice of restaurants. **33**

The Bay of Palma

Two sweeps of white sand made Palma's magnificent bay a summer magnet, and the resorts that spread out along them gave Mallorca a name for cheap and cheerful holidays. That picture was always over-simplified: there's a of choice, including the most luxurious and expensive. But the millions come year after year, knowing what they want. The two arms of the bay still reach out to embrace them.

East: Platja de Palma

The south-eastern shore of the bay runs through former fishing villages to the beach resort and yacht harbour of Ca'n Pastilla, almost at the end of the airport runway. Then, without a break, come Las Maravillas and S'Arenal, a 7-kilometre (4-mi.) strip of hotels, fast food, loud bars and discos, British pubs and German beerhalls. Restaurants range from the "English-Owned—No Oil Used" type to a few rather good Mallorcan ones. The sea-front and the narrow streets behind can be a riot of fun—and noise—all summernight long. You don't come here for peace and quiet. Whether you've slept off the effects or not, next day you'll be picking your way across the broad beach to the blue water, tiptoeing through another sea... of tightly packed bodies.

West Side of the Bay

To the west of Palma, **Cala Major** ("great cove") has been a holiday centre since long before the package tour boom. The royal family has a summer home here and uses it as a base for sailing. At Sant Agustí and Illetes you can swim off the rocks or the small sandy beaches—some man-made—and stay at hotels with an old-established air, where you'll wake to the sound of waves. Alternation of rock and sand continues past more-exclusive Bendinat to Portals Nous where apartment blocks cluster on the slopes above the water. The glamorous-looking marina of Puerto Punta Portals was ambitiously carved out of the cliffs.

Sandy beaches start again at Costa d'En Blanes, home of **Marineland** with its dolphin displays, and Palma Nova, which blends imperceptibly into big, brash **Magalluf**. Here the ranks of hotels and apart-

Magnet for the masses: Magalluf's gently sloping sandy beach.

ment blocks mark another burst of facilities for mass tourism, provided with brilliant efficiency, if not much regard for aesthetics. The wide sandy beach, sloping safely into the sea, can hardly be seen in summer for browning bodies. Bars a block long, discos built like airport terminals, restaurants with menus in eight languages from Finnish to French, go-karts, waterslides, a Wild West show—you name it, Magalluf has it. Except tranquillity. For that, you have around 95 per cent of the rest of the island to choose from.

West of Magalluf, the road leads towards the golf course. To the south, the once-quiet cove of Cala Vinjes has been practically covered with concrete in a wild orgy of overbuilding. Continue through pine woods to the Casino de Mallorca and by narrow winding lanes to the pretty coves and beaches of **Portals Vells**. Here in the cliffs, you'll find huge rock-cut caverns dating from Roman times or earlier, and enlarged over the centuries. In one, an altar carved out of the soft stone is said to have been made by Italian sailors in gratitude for surviving a shipwreck. Sadly, it's been vandalized in recent years. Boats make the short excursion, from the pier on Magalluf beach. Not far south of Portals Vells, you can hike down to one more cove, the very quiet Cala Figuera (don't confuse it with various others of the same name). Then the road is blocked: the end of the peninsula is a military zone.

The Western Tip

King Juan Carlos likes to drive his guests round a circuit to the west of Palma, showing them the stunning scenery of coast and mountains. You might take a leaf out of the royal tour book.

The main road bypasses the resorts of the Bay of Palma and meets the sea again at **Santa Ponça**, where a cross on a headland marks the landing place of King Jaume I and his Catalan army in 1229, beginning the campaign to recapture Mallorca from the Moors. Dramatic reliefs on the base of the memorial depict the event. Sandy beaches and the sheltered bay now attract another sort of invasion, although some say Santa Ponça is a decibel or two less noisy than the loudest resorts. It boasts one of the widest ranges of sports, and keeps going out of season, too, with an older clientele. So does neighbouring Peguera, with its similar facilities.

The pleasant tree-shaded beaches of Cala Fornells are still picturesque although hotels and clusters of villas press closely round. Camp de Mar, with its big, plain hotels on the next inlet has more sand but less charm. A twisting little scenic road leads to **Port d'Andratx**, a broad, wonderfully sheltered bay that is home to more yachts than fishing boats these days. The old harbour area on the south side keeps its traditional appearance, though a closer look reveals a string of restaurants, and the slopes facing it across the water are now encrusted with villas and apartments. You can swim off the rocks; lack of a sandy beach has kept the big hotels away, which is just fine with those who have known and loved the place for years. A short drive, a brisk walk or a morning jog takes you 3 kilometres (2 mi.) to the **Cap de Sa Mola**, most southwesterly point on the island, with superb views of sheer cliffs and shining sea.

The main road inland leads to the port's "twin" town of **Andratx**, all brown stone houses and a maze of little one-way streets that puts foreign motorists to the test. Many Mallorcan towns (Pollença and Sóller are other examples) are built like this one, several miles from the sea that brought them trade and fish. The main reason for the inland site was to put some distance between the town and marauding pirates, though most of the smaller harbours had little room for building anyway. Topped by its fortress-like 13th-century church, Andratx seems to ignore the rest of the world, and most traffic simply passes by on the edge of town.

From Andratx, a dead-end road leads to the coast at **San Telm** (Sant Elm), a former fishing village which doesn't try too hard to be a resort. The view offshore from its mostly stony little beaches is dominated by the island of **Sa Dragonera**, subject of a long legal battle between would-be developers and conservationists. It seems likely that the lizards which gave the island its name will be left in peace.

You can head back to Palma from Andratx by country roads, passing through farmland and orchards and the prosperous towns of Capdella and Calvia. More adventurously, if you don't mind more hairpin bends than an Alpine pass, go the longer way round through Galilea and Puigpunyent, stopping to take in the views.

North-west: Coast and Mountains

Mallorca's most dramatic stretch of coastline faces the Spanish mainland. Mountains sweep down to the sea so steeply here that there are few points of access and only one harbour and port of any size. The road winds along clifftops from one vertigo-inducing viewpoint to the next, frequently giving up any attempt to stay close to the water and meandering into the mountains instead. North of Andratx, it reaches the first of a succession of **miradors**, high places with a commanding prospect of the coast. Some of them are still crowned with ancient watchtowers, where lookouts anxiously scanned the sea for pirate ships and signalled warnings to the next point along the chain. If you can, make the trip early in the morning, or you'll be part of a procession from one parking spot to the next.

At **Estellencs**, an ancient town amid terraces and orange groves, you can walk or drive down a track to a little fishing cove. Back on the main road, take in one of the best views, from the snail-shaped tower of **Ses Animes** ("the spirits"). Around the town of **Banyalbufar,** the hillsides have been

tamed since Moorish times into some of the finest terraces on the island. A narrow lane twists down to a rocky cove and small beach, and another, even longer and more serpentine, reaches the sea at Es Canonge. Facilities in the area are few but despite this—or because of it— the few hotels that exist have

Centuries of toil have transformed Banyalbufar's rocky hillsides.

their quiet adherents, and villas are going up.

North of Banyalbufar, the road turns its back on the coast for a while. Just off it, in the direction of Esporles, you'll find **La Granja**, a cross between a stately home, a traditional farmhouse, a craft centre and a living museum of rural Mallorcan life. In the shade of the massive outbuildings and cellars, you may see a potter or blacksmith at work. You can sample local wines, sweet and **39** fortified, or orange and lemon cordials. Here, too, are children's play areas, gardens to stroll through, geese and ducks, sheep with their bells tinkling musically, donkey rides and sometimes country dancing. Fountains and ponds are fed by springs first channelled by the Moors. Inside the house, everything looks estate-made, and it probably was: the furniture is folksy and walls are painted to look as if they have been papered. Friendly staff, some in traditional dress, demonstrate the weaving of cloth, carpets and ribbons, lacemaking and embroidery. The estate belonged to Cistercian monks before it came to the Fortuny family, which still owns it.

Valldemossa is a town transformed by the short visit, over a century and a half ago, of French writer George Sand and her lover, Frédéric Chopin. Their few weeks here in the winter of 1838–39 seem to have been essentially miserable: Chopin was ill, the weather was wet and cold and bad for his chest, and George Sand despised the local people, describing them in her book *A Winter in Majorca* as "barbarians, thieves and monkeys". They can't have thought too highly of her, either—a scandalous woman who smoked,

wore trousers and had left her husband to live with another man.

But their stay was enough to create a cult. Now, busloads of visitors are brought almost daily to see the couple's lodgings in the former Carthusian monastery **Sa Cartuja.** The monks had been expelled in 1835 and some of their cells sold as holiday apartments, in a foretaste of the fashion of the future. The word "cells" perhaps gives a false idea; in fact, each is a suite of three rooms with a private garden. The two cells that the lovers rented are now a museum dedicated to them, with original manuscripts, Chopin's death mask and his pianos—one local and one sent from Paris which, to compound his frustrations, didn't arrive until shortly before he left. You'll see, too, the massive church, the monks' pharmacy with its collection of 18th-century jars, their library and the guests' dining room. (The monks ate alone in their cells, served through hatches, consuming simple fare that supposedly accounted for their famous longevity.) There's a dull municipal museum in the monastery, and the adjacent "Palace of King Sanç" has only a very tenuous link with the 14th-century Mallorcan king.

The daytime tourist influx rather swamps Valldemossa, but by the evening the town is able to sit back and breathe again, and the cool early mornings can be idyllic. At least as significant to Mallorcans as the Chopin connection is the fact that Valldemossa was the birthplace, in 1531, of their own saint, Catalina Thomàs. You can see statues of her in churches all over the island, and coloured tiles bearing her image decorate nearly every doorway in Valldemossa.

There couldn't be a greater contrast to George Sand's negative reaction than the lifelong love affair of the Austrian Archduke Ludwig Salvator (or Luis Salvador) with the Balearics and their people. He first saw this coast from his steam yacht; in 1870 he bought the estate of **Son Marroig** (just outside Deià). The house, open to visitors, is filled with his collections, photographs and the books he wrote, including a study of the Balearics in six huge volumes. If you are lucky, you may be welcomed and shown round by the granddaughter of the archduke's secretary, who inherited the estate. Afterwards, walk in the gardens and take in the bird's-eye view from the cliff-edge temple built for Salvator

out of Italian marble. The rocky headland, **Na Foradada**, jutting into the sea hundreds of feet below, is pierced by a remarkable 18-metre-wide (60-ft.) natural window. If you feel energetic, take the half-hour's walk down to the sea and the little landing stage where the archduke and his guests used to come ashore. A swim off the rocks will refresh you for the hard march uphill.

Nowadays they would be called "ex-pats", these foreigners who came to Mallorca and stayed. **Deià**, a pretty hilltop town of honey-coloured stone, has attracted plenty, ever since Robert Graves, the poet and author of *I, Claudius*, came to live here with Laura Riding in 1929, followed by a strange coterie of admirers. In later life he became the Grand Old Man of Deià, fierce in his defence of it against touristic exploitation. It comes as a shock to learn that in his early days here he tried to set himself up as a property developer, intending to build a hotel. One or two mansions in the vicinity have been turned in recent years into country house hotels, which tend to be full from the moment they open in spring. Summer brings film producers and rock stars who take houses in the town. **41**

Daytime tourists see little of this: Deià presents mainly closed doors to them as they make their way to the top of the hill. There, in the cemetery near the church, a simple cement slab bears the inscription: *Robert Graves, Poeta, 1895–1985.*

It's a long twisting drive down to Deià's tiny fishing cove, with ladder-like ramps coming out of boathouses set into the cliffs. A snack bar and beach café open in summer, but the rocky shore can be choked with seaweed. If you take a picnic, watch out: the place is alive with hungry cats.

At Sóller and its seaside twin **Port de Sóller**, the cliffs and mountains at last relent. The biggest bay on the north-west coast makes a fine harbour, but is so enclosed that both the

Chopin and George Sand found a winter hideaway in Valldemossa.

water and the beach can be dirty. Sheltered slopes a few miles inland are covered in groves of olive, lemon, orange and almond trees, with the highest mountain on the island, **Puig Major** (1,445 m./ 4,740 ft.), as a rugged backdrop. Sóller is a busy, prosperous town that claims like many others that it was the birthplace of Columbus. Trams—some open-sided and fancifully said to be transplanted San Francisco cable cars—run every half-hour through lemon groves to Port de Sóller, continuing along the waterfront there. That isn't all there is to delight rail fans. Sóller and Palma are linked by narrow-gauge **electric railway.** Five times a day (six on Sundays), polished wooden trains make the hour-long journey in each direction through orchards and spectacular mountain scenery, stopping at Son Sardina and Bunyola. The 10.40 a.m. "special" from Palma makes an extra scenic halt above Sóller.

If Sóller and especially its port look French, there's a reason. In past centuries, they were cut off by the mountains from the rest of the island, so that trade with France became a mainstay. Growing holiday business has brought new hotels and apartments around the bay, mercifully without quite spoiling the look of the waterfront. Fishermen still bring in their catches to the harbour, and right opposite, a line of restaurants suit most budgets, though fish is never cheap.

Two pretty villages near Sóller have enticed foreigners to buy houses and tourists to come and look. **Fornalutx** is a jewel of warm stone that looks as if it intends to win a prize as "best-kept place in Mallorca". Some of its neat cobbled streets climb in steep steps up the hillside. Similarly set among orange trees and wild flowers, **Biniraix** is only a short stroll away down narrow lanes.

The authorities felt that the road from Palma to Sóller, with dozens of hairpin bends and the 496-metre (1,627-ft.) pass, the Coll de Sóller, was impeding commerce and development. Probably so, and no doubt with the approval of many who liked the area as it was. In spite of vigorous protests, plans were approved for a road tunnel under the mountains, and digging began in 1990.

On the southern slope, right opposite the tunnel entrance, the seigneurial mansion and gardens of **Alfabia** were once the country estate of the Moorish Vizier of Palma, though they have been much altered **43** since. These days, the cisterns, fountains and irrigation channels are rather run down, but the flowing water and shaded walks, turkeys feeding under fig trees, birds singing among exotic plants and inviting places to sit down and have a cool drink nevertheless exert a gentle attraction. The house is like a forgotten palace, full of neglected treasures. Don't miss the huge wooden 14th-century chair in the print room, called by one expert "the most important antique in Mallorca". Old farm carts are parked in the courtyard; the fierce-sounding dogs on guard are on leashes, you'll be glad to see. In the gatehouse, look up. The ceiling, though restored and often repainted, is basically a 13th-century Moorish creation.

The hilly country to the east of here, reached via Bunyola, is a favourite with walkers based at the little village of **Orient** or coming for a day's change from the coast. A massive mountain crag 822 metres (2,700 ft.) high is crowned by the **Castell d'Alaró**, a ruined fortress dating from the time of the Moors. You can make the long walk from Orient, or drive most of the way towards the summit up narrow and tortuous lanes, starting a little north of Alaró. The higher they climb, the

rougher these tracks get, so you'll need an agile vehicle, not too big, low-slung or heavily laden. The final ascent has to be made on foot up rocky paths—wear your rubber-soled shoes. The gates and walls of the castle still guard the clifftop, and the views are as thrilling as any on Mallorca. Your sense of achievement may be dented by finding a restaurant on the mountaintop—or you may just be glad of a cool drink.

Forced away from the sea by the steep terrain, the main road north from Sóller climbs over the high pass of Coll de Puig Major and past the dams and reservoirs of Cuber and **Gorg Blau**. By the roadside near the second of these stands a battered old stone column, rescued, so a sign proclaims, from the flooding of the valley. Near the dam, a little road sets off to the coast. Its name, **Sa Calobra** ("the snake"), gives a hint of the 13 kilometres (8 mi.) of hairpin bends which have become a tourist attraction in themselves, starting with one loop so exaggerated that the road passes under itself in a knot. If you are driving, early morning is the time to avoid the traffic. The light will be better, too, on the strangely fluted and sharp edges of eroded limestone, interspersed with ancient

La Moreneta, *venerated stone statue of the Virgin and Child at Lluc monastery.*

gnarled olive trees. As a reward at the bottom of the winding road, Cala de Sa Calobra has a restaurant and bars and a pebbly beach, but the main objective is one of the wonders of Mallorca, the deep gorges of the **Torrent de Pareis** ("the twins"). Tunnels, enlarged from natural crevices in the rock, burrow through to the riverbed where it widens into a natural theatre (concerts are given on some summer evenings). The beautiful little beach at the point where it meets the sea can be crowded, so if you want more solitude, and if the river is as dry as usual, walk back along it between cliffs hundreds of feet high. If you can arrange to be met, carry a drink and a snack and make the demanding four-hour hike all the way down the gorge **45** from the main road near Escorca.

At the **Monasteri de Lluc** foreign visitors are usually outnumbered for once by local people, for this is Mallorca's favourite place of pilgrimage. It was founded in the 13th century, but the massive buildings you see now date from the 17th and 18th. The islanders come to see and pray to a statue of the Madonna and Child, called **La Moreneta** ("little brown one") because of the dark colour of its stone surface. A dozen conflicting legends have grown up about its origins and adventurous history. One says it was found here and taken to a nearby church. During the night the statue disappeared, only to be rediscovered back at the spot where it had originally been found. Twice more this happened, as though the statue willed that it should not be moved. So a chapel was built over the site and later the monastery grew up. You'll find the statue behind the high altar; the diamonds, emeralds and pearls set into the two crowns have been donated over the years by Mallorcans. If you can attend mass in the church, you may hear the famous Lluc boys' choir, Es Blavets ("the blue ones"), named after the colour of their cassocks.

North-east: Capes and Bays

Plenty of arrivals at Palma's airport make a beeline for the north-east coast and its two great sandy bays.

Port de Pollença is the kind of place that gives Mallorca a good name—a perfectly sheltered, gently sloping sandy beach, a spectrum of hotels, *hostals,* apartments and villas, a choice of restaurants and some not-too-rowdy nightlife. These days, there are more luxury craft than fishing vessels in the harbour, and flotillas of windsurfers in the bay.

If you don't have your own yacht, go by excursion boat round the spectacular cliffs of **Cap de Formentor**, the narrow headland that juts out 13 kilometres (8 mi.) on the north side of the bay. By land, take the beautifully engineered road along the cape, pausing where everyone else does (but it's still worth doing) at the giddy viewpoint not far from Port de Pollença. Most boats and cars stop at the pine-shaded beach (Platja de Formentor or Cala Pi). It's a favourite spot for a picnic,

On the road to Cap de Formentor, a vertigo-inducing viewpoint.

swimming, and taking a look at the luxurious Hotel Formentor and its gardens. This dream of the German-Argentinian Adan Diehl was inaugurated in 1930, and promoted a fashion among the famous for relaxing on Mallorca. But the timing unluckily corresponded with the onset of the Great Depression and the approaching Civil War. In seven years its creator was bankrupt and the hotel closed. Given a new lease of life in 1954, it quickly re-established its old prestige.

Situated a few miles from the sea, to make it harder for corsairs to attack, **Pollença** was founded in 1230 after the defeat of the Moors. The name comes from the old Roman capital of Mallorca, Pollentia, whose site was some miles away near Alcúdia. Until 1802 the town belonged to the Order of the Knights of St. John, like Valletta in Malta, and many handsome stone buildings in the centre date from their time.

Whether Pollença's bridge labelled *Pont Roman* is really Roman is questionable, but the locals say so, and the tourists believe what they are told and photograph it. Most of the visitors head to the parish church in the town centre to make the climb up the 365 cypress-lined shallow steps of the **Calvari**

to the tiny church at the top. (There's also a road up, passing the 14 Stations of the Cross.)

From the top of the Calvari steps, you can look across to the much higher **Ermita del Puig de María.** Find the correct little turning south of town, and you can drive most of the way up, negotiating some alarming hairpin bends where you'll pray not to meet anything coming down. Eventually the road gives out, and the last ten minutes of the rewarding ascent to the fortified monastery at the summit are made on foot.

One of the best walks on Mallorca can be made only on a Saturday. Pollença is again the starting point, but this time you'll head north, by the narrow road towards **Ternelles**. Cars can go just a short distance, past some attractive houses, before reaching a checkpoint where they have to turn back. But one day a week, the landowners open their "frontier" to allow walkers only to go through (even cyclists are prohibited). The route follows the gorge of the Torrent de Ternelles at first, then turns off to head for the ruined **Castell del Rei**, first built by the Moors on a soaring crag 500 metres (1,640 ft.) above the sea. Another rough track leads down to the shore at Cala Castell. The whole walk covers about 13 kilometres (8 mi.).

After cruising under the cliffs of Cap de Formentor, excursion launches may put into **Cala Sant Vicenç**, twin sandy coves with brilliant blue water, and hotels and villas situated on the clifftop.

Less dramatic than the Formentor peninsula, **Cap d'es Pinar** separates the Bay of Pollença from the still bigger Bay of Alcúdia. You can't go to the end—it's a military zone—but several little rocky coves and beaches make the Cap worth exploring. Astride the neck of land between the two bays stands the ancient walled town of **Alcúdia**. Too close to the sea for safety from raids, it must have been dependent on its impressive fortifications, rebuilt in the 16th century. The church of Sant Jaume is even more fortress-like than most, actually forming the southern bastion in the walls.

Beyond the road that circles the town, you can see the low ruins remaining from Roman Pollentia. They're not impressive as such sites go, but some fine relics excavated there are now displayed in the little **museum**, a beautifully restored old building opposite Sant Jaume church. Just off the road leading from Alcúdia to its port stands the **Roman theatre**, hewn out of solid rock in the 1st century B.C. The slope is quite gentle, so it wasn't sufficient just to cut steps for the seats: grooves had to be made between the rows, or the spectators' knees would have been under their chins. The site was later used as a cemetery.

From a small fishing harbour, **Port d'Alcúdia** has evolved into an all-purpose port for commercial, naval and pleasure craft (there's a big yacht marina) and a summer resort. Restaurants and discos have multiplied. Hotels and apartment blocks have spread ever further round the bay to form an almost unbroken ribbon 10 kilometres (6 mi.) long.

Behind the coast, Llac Gran ("big lake") and the precious wetlands of **S'Albufera** are a haven for birdlife. Drainage schemes in the 19th century ran into such problems that the British company responsible for building a network of canals, paths and bridges—still to be seen today—went bust thereafter. Some 800 hectares (2,000 acres) have now been designated a *Parc Natural* (nature reserve) where you can walk or cycle among the reeds, looking for some of the 200 species of birds that have been spotted here.

49

East Coast: Coves and Caves

Tiny harbours, some no more than a half-hidden cleft in the cliffs, alternate with larger bays along Mallorca's eastern shore. A dwindling few are almost undiscovered, others carry on fishing while welcoming an annual invasion of visitors. Some sheltered marina developments are millionaires' rows of sleek white status symbols. Here and there, huge clusters of villas turn from ghost town to boom town as soon as summer arrives.

Cala Ratjada is just about as far as you can get from Palma without having to take to the water. But the water is what most people are here for, whether it's the fishermen or the holiday-makers who vastly outnumber them, for the harbour now is the focus of a lively resort. Check with the local tourist information office to arrange a visit to the **Juan March Sculpture Garden**, with works by Rodin, Henry Moore, Barbara Hepworth and many modern Spanish masters.

Sand beaches are close by at Cala Guya and Cala Molto, and there's a fine view of the coast from the lighthouse on Cap Capdepera. If it's clear, you'll be able to see Menorca. On the 271-metre (889-ft.) peak of Jaumell, the next headland to the north, there used to be a semaphore station for signalling between the islands, in the days before radio and telephone cables (and when the air was clearer). The cape takes its name from **Capdepera** where you can walk round the battlements of the 14th-century castle on the hill above the town.

Five miles from the sea, the country town of **Artà** seems far removed from tourism. No hotels, but prosperity brought by the holiday business has nevertheless rubbed off. Here as elsewhere, money has been spent on upkeep: the place has probably never looked better. Steps lead up by a Way of the Cross to the fortified church of Sant Salvador, where you get a fine view of the town, hills and coast. A painting inside depicts the killing of Ramón Llull while he was trying to convert the Muslims of North Africa, though whether this actually happened, or whether he died of old age at home, is a matter of conjecture. A rare surviving Civil War monument has been pointedly amended to commemorate *all* the dead.

A sign pointing down a side road in the southern outskirts of Artà says simply "Talaiot", but it leads to one of the most important megalithic settlements in Mallorca, **Ses Paisses**. Hidden among trees, the foundations of its rough buildings are ringed by walls of huge stones, with one massive gateway still intact. The site dates from around 1200–800 B.C. and was probably continuously occupied throughout Roman times.

Some distance away on the coast, Artà has given its name to the limestone caves called **Coves d'Artà**. The entrance, a great arch in the overhanging cliffs, is at the top of a long flight of steps. Then more steps (this is not a place for the immobile) take you down into vast chambers full of stalactites and stalagmites looking like groves of trees or piles of broccoli. One slender pillar has climbed to 22 metres (72 ft.) and has only a little way to go to reach the roof—but don't hold your breath, it will take 5,000 years. Coloured lights and Bach organ music point up the name given to the lowest level, "The Inferno". Jules Verne is said to have been inspired by a visit here to write *Journey to the Centre of the Earth*.

The road to Canyamel, a sandy bay shaded by pines, is highlighted by the restored 14th-century **Torre de Canyamel** and Mallorca's most easterly golf course. South-facing Costa dels Pins has an exclusive air, but the same could never be said of Cala Millor, a long stretch of sand and rocks backed by a solid wall of hotels and apartments, plus all the facilities generated by mass British tourism. Adjoining Cala Bona is somewhat quieter. Behind the coast, Son Servera has a Friday market and some real Mallorcan life.

How about a safari as a change from the beach? The **Reserva Africana** has a fair selection of wildlife—antelopes, elephants, rhino and ostriches. You drive slowly through the 40-hectare (100-acre) park, and although there are no dangerous predators, you are requested to stay in the car. Close the windows, too, if baboons or monkeys come near: they've been fed by people in the past and might jump right in to see what you've got. A little zoo houses mainly young animals in reasonably open conditions.

S'Illot, Cala Moreia and Cala Morlanda are growing into standard big white clusters of villas and hotels, by a white sand beach, but neighbouring **Porto Cristo** is something special. It's a popular holiday place, but fishermen still set out from the old port, which is con-

cealed and sheltered from the sea by an S-bend inlet (unfortunately too narrow for the water and beach to be flushed clean). In 1936, after the start of the Civil War, the republicans landed a large force here in an unsuccessful attempt to take Mallorca from the Nationalists.

Two groups of caves in the vicinity of Porto Cristo make a cool change from the beach—and attract a procession of tour buses at peak times. The highly commercial **Coves del Drac** (Caves of the Dragon) south of the port meander for more than a mile of huge chambers and spectacular formations with fanciful names (such as Fairy's Theatre or Diana's Bath). The highlight is the 177-metre-long (581-ft.) underground lake named after Edouard-Alfred Martel, the French speleologist who explored the caves in 1896. Here, the typical *son et lumière* show that most caves go in for is capped by a kitsch performance of... but let's not spoil the surprise. A little way inland, the smaller **Coves dels Hams** are named after the fish-hook shapes of some of the stalactites. There's a succession of chambers with beautiful formations, a much smaller lake than the one at Coves del Drac and, again, no escape

from the coloured-light-and-music show. For an inland excursion, Manacor and Petra (see p. 58) are not far away and worth exploring.

The perfect harbour of **Porto Colom** has been surprisingly little changed by the tourism boom. Boathouses in a row line the waterfront below the

Pretty harbours like Cala Figuera dot Mallorca's south-east coast. Getting around is easier by water than by road.

prettily painted houses of the fishermen. Commercial activity and the very narrow outlet to the sea mean that the water and the beaches inside the harbour can get dirty, but there are sea beaches close by to the north and south. No-one else may agree, but the locals claim that Columbus came from here. At least the name of the port is on their side, which is more, they **53** point out, than Genoa can say. For an inland excursion head to Felanitx and on to the hilltop castle of Santueri (see p. 59).

Cala d'Or came early to the resort business, and it has evolved into a huge complex, with all the facilities and watersports you could ask for, though the small beaches become overloaded in summer. You can get lost in the network of new roads—it seems as if they're getting ready for the 21st century. The yachts and cruisers tied up at the marina have an expensive air of "keeping up with the Joneses" (or perhaps the Schmidts, for this is a favourite spot with German visitors). How expensive? If you have to ask, you're out of your depth. In contrast, nearby **Porto Petro** still looks like a traditional fishing village, even though it's taken over in summer by a Nordic invasion.

The practically undeveloped Cala Mondragó may stay that way by order of the regional government, which is alarmed by the spectre of unchecked building all round the coast. One of the gems that first attracted visitors to this part, **Cala Figuera** is still delightful, with neat houses and unpretentious boats lining its Y-shaped inlet.

The South

Few visitors knew anything of Mallorca's deep south until recent years. The long sandy beach of **Es Trenc**, for example, was left to the islanders to enjoy on weekends, though a few pioneering nudists established themselves at one end near Ses Covetes. The picture is changing a little. Roads from Campos and Santanyi have been improved and a few signposts erected; even the nudists have been made official. But it seems that development won't be permitted. Es Trenc is for those who don't want any manmade facilities.

Inland, **Ses Salines** takes its name from the local salt flats and ponds, where bird-watchers gather in the spring to see the migrants that make this their first landfall on the way north from Africa. A big investment of money and effort on a 15-hectare (37-acre) site has created **Botanicactus**, a botanic garden specializing in cacti. Its 500 varieties, spiny, fluffy, tall and short, and 200 types of succulents come from all the dry regions of the world.

Colònia de Sant Jordi was one of the more half-hearted attempts at a resort, with a rather shadeless and windblown look. The harbour of

Campos, nearby, serves as the starting point for excursions to **Cabrera,** an island usually visible 17 kilometres (11 mi.) to the south, which got its name from the herds of goats that grazed on it from ancient times. Visits are limited to parties of bird-watchers or zoologists and excursion groups, who get an hour and a half ashore for a short walk, a swim and a picnic. Cova Blava is Cabrera's "Blue Grotto", reached only from the sea; excursion boats sometimes make the trip.

Five kilometres (3 mi.) inland from Cala Pi, you'll find the most remarkable prehistoric settlement in Mallorca, **Capocorp Vell.** You may not find it easily, though. The friendly family who look after the site say that people often arrive breathing sighs of relief after searching the maze of narrow lanes that criss-cross this flat landscape. More clues: it's 6 kilometres (4 mi.) from Cap Blanc on the most direct road towards Llucmajor, which is 12 kilometres (7 mi.) away.

From as early as 1200 B.C., massive stones were cut and hauled into place to build a village. The remains you see now are over 200 metres (650 ft.) long, but traces of other buildings cover a much wider area. The five *talaiots*

(three round towers, two square) may have been added somewhat later. Climb to the top of one for a good view of the site and, on a clear day, the island of Cabrera. This is a strange and impressive place: you can still walk through doorways into complete rooms. Agile explorers can wriggle several yards down the winding passage under one of the towers (take a light); it leads eventually to what was presumably a burial chamber for tribal chiefs. Remarkably, its olive-wood roof is still partially intact.

The Centre

The local name, **Es Pla** ("the plain"), doesn't sound promising. Certainly not enticing enough to slow down fun-seekers as they rush across the middle of Mallorca to get to their favourite piece of coast and avoid the heat. But make an early start, or choose a cooler day, and rewards are waiting. For the growing numbers of spring and autumn visitors who come to cycle, walk, and spot birds and wild flowers, the plain is just what they fancy.

The main towns, on the busiest roadways, are not Mallorca's most attractive ones. But take any back road and you'll discover little villages **55** untouched by tourism, or see farmers still ploughing with horses. Stretching from the highlands of the north-west to the hills of the south-east, the plain is not as flat as its name implies. Peaks suddenly stick up, crowned with an ancient monastery or castle ramparts, where there's a wonderful silence and views over orchards and fields that make you feel as if you're flying.

On the busy road north-east from Palma, the palatial former convent at **Santa María del Camí** now houses shops selling the locally made wines and leather goods, and a folk and archaeological museum. Turn off the main road to find the attractive part of **Binissalem**, centre of Mallorca's wine production. North-east of the town, a leisure park offers playgrounds, a pool with a waterslide, and a wax museum of characters famous in Mallorcan history, from Stone-Age slingers to George Sand.

The face of **Inca**, centre of the leather industry (with several factory outlets), is disfigured by ugly apartment blocks. But it's worth exploring the narrow streets and visiting the monastery cloisters of Sant Francesc before picking one of the old wine-cellar restaurants for some traditional Mallorcan food. Inca's Thursday market sprawls through the streets; it's well known and tour buses come in flotillas, though the goods are much the same as in markets anywhere else on the island.

Rich farmland surrounds **Sa Pobla**, and some of the massed ranks of windmills still pump water from wells first dug by the Moors a thousand years ago. Plastic pipes and plastic sheeting have transformed agriculture here, so that early fruit and vegetables and new

Riot of wild red poppies in central plain Es Pla; grapes destined for Felanitx's palatable wines.

potatoes can be rushed to northern Europe.

The pretty country town of **Muro** has a fine example of a Mallorcan arcaded church, and an elegant town house around a courtyard and garden has been restored as the home of the ethnology section of the **Museu de Mallorca**. Although short on labelling, the displays of traditional tools, old carriages and pottery are worth seeing, and the house itself is the star exhibit.

Sineu, practically at the centre of the island, is the site King Jaume II chose to build a palace; it survives, much altered, as a convent. The rail way which now runs only from Palma to Inca used to come to Sineu and on to Manacor and Artà, and the track is still there, albeit overgrown or buried, for most of the way.

One little inland town, **Petra**, is quite typical of the plain, with warm brown stone houses fronting directly onto quiet streets. Here was born, in 1713, Junipero Serra, a Franciscan friar with a better claim than anyone to be called the founder of California. When an expedition was sent from Mexico by order of King Carlos III in 1768, his task was to set up the chain of missions along the Pacific coast that eventually grew into today's cities of San Diego, Los Angeles, San José and San Francisco. You can visit **Casa Serra**, the house where he was born. It has a low second storey (note the little four-poster bed upstairs) and a pocket-sized garden. If it's closed, a woman who lives nearby will bring the key. She'll open the **Museu Serra**, too, where you can see tributes from today's Californians and paintings and photographs of the missions the friar founded. They're also shown in tile panels along Carrer California next to the church. Serra was beatified in 1988, the status preliminary to being declared a saint.

In Mallorca, pearls don't come from oysters. They're made in **Manacor**, largest town after Palma but less than one-tenth the size. The place has an industrial look, and most traffic gratefully takes the road that bypasses the centre. Interesting old defensive towers and some fine stonework are not enough to compensate for the trouble of reaching them, except perhaps on a quiet Sunday morning. But the pearl-makers have enterprisingly set up shop on the highway, and you can tour their factories too. At the busiest times you'll be part of a production line yourself—

thousands troop through every day. In the century-old process, glass beads are coated with a lustrous glaze made from powdered fish-scales and resin. After this is baked on, it's hard to tell the result from a real pearl.

At **Felanitx,** the honey-coloured church dates in part from the 13th century. Its lovely west front, at the top of a huge, elegant flight of steps, is from the 17th. In the street alongside, a stone tablet commemorates a tragedy: during an Easter procession in 1844, the collapse of a wall killed no fewer than 414 people. Some unusually good pottery is made in the town, and it used to be renowned also for its cartographers—who Mallorcans claim furnished Columbus with maps—when they're not claiming Columbus himself.

Felanitx is the starting point for a trip to **Castell de Santueri,** a ruined hilltop castle that was fortified by every ruler from Roman times to the 17th century. Take the exhilarating walk round the ramparts—there's nothing between you and a dizzying precipice. The views of the coast are superb, and on a rare clear day you'll see Menorca and Ibiza too.

On the next hill to the north—unless you're a serious walker you'll have to go back through Felanitx to reach it—the **Puig de Sant Salvador** is the site of a hermitage and one of Mallorca's most important places of pilgrimage. In the church, look behind the altar at the Gothic statue of the Virgin Mary, backed by an alabaster panel of blond angels. In the gatehouse you'll see a 5-metre-long (17-ft.) Gothic panel of the Last Supper, in wood and plaster.

Suddenly rearing up out of the flat lands south of Algaida, the 542-metre-high (1,778-ft.) **Puig de Randa** is topped by a monastery founded in the 13th century by the Mallorcan sage, Ramón Llull. Two more monasteries are tucked into the shelter of cliffs on the way up. They're all reached by the same narrow, twisting road, and it's worth stopping at each as you make the ascent, if only to see the panorama of the plain unfold. **Llucmajor**, the attractive town just south of Randa, was the site of the battle of 1349 in which Jaume III was defeated and killed by the forces of his cousin, Pedro IV of Aragón. It's a sad date for many islanders, for it brought to an end, after only 120 years, the story of the independent kingdom of Mallorca.

59

Menorca

Menorca is one-fifth the area of its neighbour, with a tenth the population and the same small fraction of visitors, but don't think of it as smaller in any other way. It's one of the best-kept secrets in the western Mediterranean; you might suspect those who love it of deliberately keeping quiet. One local author called a book about his home *Wind and Stones,* which is hardly complimentary; in truth, this "little" island is unique and enchanting.

The geography appears simple enough: the capital and biggest town, Mahón (Maó in the *Menorquí* dialect), is at the eastern end, and the former capital Ciutadella at the western. Like a fish's backbone, one main road links them, with places on the north or south coasts connected to it by a mere handful of other roads. A detailed map will show a maze of tiny lanes and tracks as well,

but even so, many coves and beaches can be reached only by walking. Scientists explain the great contrasts between the northern and southern halves in terms of the geological formation of the island, but you'll see the effects in the landscape. The north is greener, lusher and indented by big bays; the south is a giant's rockery, riddled with caves and dotted with prehistoric marvels, its coast a succession of secret coves.

The *Menorquí* language includes a number of words picked up from the British in the 18th century. The subjects, presumably important in relations between the occupiers and the locals, tend to concentrate on carpentry, food and drink. *Neversó*, for example, is the name of a kind of plum. It comes from a comment made by Sir Richard Kane, the first British governor: "I *never saw* such plums". *Baienbai* means "by and by", *xumeca*, "shoemaker" and *quitil,* "kettle".

Favourite with fleets for centuries: Mahón's magnificent anchorage.

Mahón (Maó) 💼

"The best ports in the Mediterranean—June, July, August and Mahón", said the 16th-century Venetian admiral Andrea Doria, implying that outside the good sailing months of summer, a fleet couldn't do better than shelter here. The 6-kilometre-long (4-mi.) deepwater harbour, guarded by forts at its mouth and shielded from winds by surrounding hills, caught the eye of the British when the Royal Navy began to operate in these waters. In 1708, during the War of the Spanish Succession, they seized the island to have use of **61** the port, and kept possession until temporarily losing it to the French in 1756. (Admiral Byng, blamed for not engaging the enemy, was later court-martialled and put before a firing squad. "From time to time," observed Voltaire, "the English shoot one of their admirals— *pour encourager les autres*.")

British occupation, on and off until 1802, left its mark. Walk through the older parts of Mahón today, and you could almost be in Georgian England. Apart from the mostly closed shutters, whole streets, including **Carrer Hannover**, look like 18th-century Plymouth or Portsmouth. But where those cities have been changed, whether by World War II bombing or urban development, Mahón has kept its elegant façades and sash windows with their original rippled glass. The deep red colour of some old houses keeps up a tradition which started when the only paint available was the anti-fouling type for ships.

Mahón is meant for walking: its impenetrable one-way system will threaten your sanity if you try to drive. The little city clusters on the cliffs above the port as well as along the quayside, and near the centre a twisting roadway and broad ceremonial steps lead from one level to the next. At the top, follow your nose to the **fish market** to see more varieties of octopus and squid than you knew existed. Next to it, housed in the vast cloisters (*Claustre del Carme*) of a former convent, are the other **markets**. Look here for some of Menorca's famous Mahón cheese, made from the milk of the cows you'll see all over the island. Varieties range from the young and mild to a hard-skinned and almost crystalline, long-matured version rivalling the best Parmesan.

Chief landmark in this area is the church of **Santa María**, a big Gothic space under a vaulted roof. It was rebuilt in the 18th century and equipped in 1810 with a massive organ which you may be lucky enough to hear played. The site was occupied by a mosque until 1287, the year the Moors were expelled by Alfonso III. His flattering statue, standing in a little square beside the church, contrives to make a reputedly weak and vicious character look like Sir Galahad. Just round the corner, the stately **Ajuntament** (Town Hall) is graced by a clock presented by the first British governor, Sir Richard Kane (1713–36). Inside, portraits of Menorcan worthies and French and

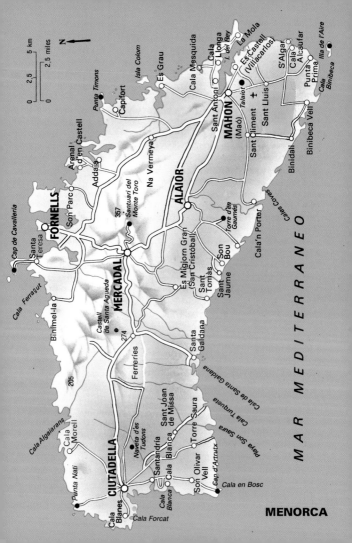

Spanish governors decorate the walls. No British governors, you'll note, and in fact no painting of Kane survives. He seems to have got on well with the Menorcans nevertheless, and he loved the island, devoting himself to improving agriculture, education and roads. Initial good relations between the islanders and the British inevitably turned sour when troops misbehaved and religious arguments blew up, and when later governors, unlike Kane, concerned themselves mainly with lining their own pockets.

A useful direction-finder in Mahón's network of narrow streets is the **Porto Sant Roc**, one of the old city gates, most of the ramparts having been levelled long ago. Follow the pedestrian streets Carrer Bastió and Carrer de Ses Moreres to the biggest square, **Plaça de S'Esplanada**, which used to be the stage for military parades. Now it's orbited by buses (most lines make a stop in the square), noisy mopeds and strollers in the early evening.

Back at the steps leading down to the port, see how the cliffs are riddled with caverns and fortifications. Beneath them, sometimes protected by nets from falling debris, stands an amazing line of disparate old buildings: ramshackle or beautifully restored, from sheds to restaurants. Near the spot where the car ferries dock, the 1892 building of **La Electrica Mahonesa** used to house an elevator system to carry people between the city and port. The **Acuarium** in the same area does have fish tanks, and you may be able to take a look in the daytime; at night it doubles as a disco. One British legacy to Menorca was a taste for gin, and the **Xoriguer distillery** established in the 18th century continues to function. You can look through big windows at copper stills bubbling away, producing a hot, colourless spirit which is poured over juniper berries to become gin.

Take a stroll along the quayside itself to see the variety of vessels tied up here, from battered trawlers to four-masters, and grey ships of the Spanish Navy at their base across the harbour. Keep going past the foot of the main steps, and you'll turn the corner into **Cala Figuera** ("English Cove" in the days of the British Navy), where pleasure craft congregate near the ships' chandlers, shops and restaurants that cater for them.

If you have time, take a **cruise** from Cala Figuera for the best views of Mahón, the harbour islands and the forts on the shore. Two of the islands once served as quarantine stations, and one of them, Americans are usually surprised to learn, was used in the 1820s for training the midshipmen of the young U.S. Navy, before the opening of the U.S. Naval Academy at Annapolis, Maryland. This unexpected connection evolved when American ships were based here during operations against the Barbary pirates of North Africa.

Whether looking from land or sea, you'll glimpse high in the hills of the north side an imposing pinkish-coloured mansion. Part-Georgian, part-Spanish style, it's called Sant Antoní but is better known as **Golden Farm**. Legend has it that Lord Nelson stayed in the house while his ship was in the harbour. Romantics go further and claim that Lady Hamilton was with him. Sad to say, although every step of Nelson's career has been tracked by his biographers, there's no record of the lovely Emma joining him here, and when in port, he seems to have preferred his bed on board to sleeping ashore. The house is privately owned, so you'll have to admire it from a distance. Admiral Cuthbert Collingwood, Nelson's friend and second-in-command at Trafalgar, who took over when

Nelson was killed, actually owned a house on the southern side of the harbour between Mahón and Es Castell. It still stands and you can stay there, for it is now a charming hotel.

Es Castell (Villacarlos), looking out over the harbour mouth, has an even more English appearance than Mahón. That's not surprising, since under the name of Georgetown it was built as the home of the British Army garrison whose main task was to man Fort San Felipe ("St. Philip's Castle", they called it) by the harbour entrance. The fort was demolished by the Spanish in 1802, supposedly to deter a British return, though the effect was to make one easier. The grass-covered foundations and colossal rock-cut caverns are still impressive. Look across the narrow strip of water to the vast fortifications opposite (still a military base) and you'll have an idea of how this side must have looked. And imagine the sight of great wooden ships of the line sailing out between them to do battle.

Excursions South of Mahón

Near the city limit, at **Trepucó** on the road south to Sant Lluis, stand Mahón's nearest *talaiot* and *taula*. Too near for their **65**

Mysterious Megaliths

You surely remember the "Flintstones", the cartoon family of cavemen? Cars, TV sets, everything made out of stone? Menorca sometimes seems a bit like that. To this day, you'll see stone dog kennels, stone drinking troughs for cattle and neat flights of projecting stone steps set into stone walls wherever you need to climb over. All those walls—they represent millennia of superhuman effort by a population that in ancient times can never have numbered more than a few thousand. But Menorca's stonemasons did more than put in a lot of work. They created remarkable buildings: hundreds of towers called *talaiots*, and burial chambers, or *navetas*, in the shape of upturned boats. The uniquely Menorcan *taula*, a massive T-shape made of two great blocks of subtly carved stone, was their masterpiece. We can only guess how they handled such weights. What were they for? Some have suggested that they held up a sort of roof structure, or that sacrifices or the bodies of the dead were exposed on top. Now, it's more generally accepted that a *taula* was itself the focus of a religious cult, the centre-piece of a temple.

own good, in fact, for the site has been damaged at various times, not least when the French army fortified it and mounted guns to fire on the British in Fort San Felipe. You'll find, as their commanders did, that the *talaiot* makes a fine observation post, but there are much more magical prehistoric places almost as close to Mahón. For contrasts between the old and new, you can hardly beat **Torelló**, a fine *talaiot* right next to the forest of landing

Curved olive-wood gates symbol-
66 *ize rural Menorca.*

lights at the north end of the airport runway. Crowned by the massive stones of a doorway—which suggests that these towers once had upper chambers—it's now topped off with a warning light for aircraft. See how the narrow lanes around here are cut into the rock, with grooves worn by cartwheels. The site continued in use until early Christian times; the outline of a basilica is visible but mostly fenced off. Not far away is a section of mosaic pavement with peacock and knot motifs. (You'll get there by taking the Sant Climent road from the airport roundabout and very soon turning right down a farm track.)

Sant Lluis, a strange town of chequerboard streets and all-white houses, was built by the French army as their headquarters in the Seven Years' War (1756–63). You'll notice the fine baroque façade of the church with its date, 1761, and the whitewashed windmill,

restored to working order. The main road now bypasses the centre and heads for the handful of resorts dotted round the south-east corner of the island.

Small sandy beaches and, in places, rocks that you can swim from, clear water and proximity to Mahón and its airport meant that this area was one of the first to be developed for holidays. At S'Algar and Cala d'Alcaufar villas cluster near a rocky shore and Punta Prima has a sandy but often messy beach. The island, Illa de l'Aire, with its lighthouse and its own subspecies of black lizards, lies close by offshore. To the west, Biniancolla and Cala Torret have pocket-handkerchief-sized beaches.

There's not much to distinguish many of these resorts, and their road networks resembling the webs of deranged spiders don't help, but **Binibeca Vell** 🧍 is something different. Taking the traditional fishing village as its inspiration, this is an intriguing "toytown" of brilliant white houses—even the roofs are white to reflect heat. Dark wooden beams and shutters and deep, shaded arches relieve the whiteness, and streets are so

One of the resorts that didn't happen: Binimel-la on Menorca's north coast. **69**

narrow you can touch both sides. In high season, when most of the villas and flats are occupied, the neighbours are so near that noise can be a problem. You'll see notices everywhere requesting "silence please".

The road makes detours inland on its way west to Binidali and Canutells, resorts more usually reached by the direct route from Mahón and the airport. **Cala'n Porter** is one of the largest, oldest-established and, in season, loudest. "Little Britain", some call it. It sprawls over a wide area, but all the facilities of a holiday town are there, and steps lead down to a sand beach. At **Cova d'en Xoroi** a cave in the steep cliff has been turned into a disco where you can dance above a vertiginous drop to the sea.

In contrast to Cala'n Porter, nearby **Cales Coves** is undeveloped. There's evidence that it was a port in Roman times, although no buildings survive. But that doesn't mean it's unpopulated today. At the end of the rough track down to the sea, various ramshackle vans and beat-up 2CVs give you a clue. Look up at the cliffs, and you'll see the openings of a hundred and more caves. They were burial chambers in the Talaiotic period; now some of them provide shelters for dropouts and backpackers. Nudists use the beach, but it can become unpleasantly choked with weeds.

Excursions North of Mahón

Expensive homes on the hillside at Cala Llonga overlook the great harbour. The tip of the peninsula, La Mola, is occupied by a naval station and the road is closed to the public. Because the opening to the sea is so narrow and tides are minimal, the water is polluted. Swimmers head for beaches further up the coast, at Cala Mesquida, which still has the look of a fishing village, and Cala Grau.

The development called Shangri-La didn't turn out to be quite as idyllic as its mythical namesake. Some 62 scattered houses and a golf course had been finished when a halt was called, amid legal and environmental controversy: the area is close to a rare little lake, **S'Albufera**, home of wildfowl and so far almost unspoilt. Echoes reached far beyond Menorca and the issue became national. "Green" interests would like to buy the houses at a knock-down price—and knock them down. The golf course is probably the only one you'll ever see that's returning to nature.

North Coast

Wild, rocky and deeply indented, much of the north coast can't be reached by road at all. The excellent main highway from Mahón runs well inland through gentler countryside of wheat and potato fields and pastures where cattle graze. The twin coves of Addaia—now a holiday village and harbour—were the site of the last British invasion in 1798, by Scottish Highland troops who must have thought these rocky hillsides covered with purple heather were just like home.

You can drive to the sea at just a few places, and inevitably some of these have grown rapidly as resorts. **Macaret** was an old fishing village, and a lot of the new building sympathetically matches the traditional look, especially around the neat little square. **Arenal d'en Castell** has a beautiful circular bay, almost enclosed and with a wide sandy beach. Intensive construction all round includes high-rise hotels, unusual on Menorca and generating summer crowds. It's the liveliest place on this side of the island, if excitement is what you're looking for.

Son Parc with its golf club, villas, shops and hotel is a completely artificial creation, near a big, flat sand beach backed by dunes. By contrast, **Fornells** (pronounced "For-nays") was and still is a real fishing village as well as a resort, with pretty houses and well-known seafood restaurants lining the waterfront near the entrance to a huge bay. Take a walk up the hill to the old watchtower for a stunning view of the harbour, the coast and the clearest of blue water. **Ses Salines**, sheltered and with shallow water, is reckoned to be one of the best places to learn to sail or windsurf.

On the next bay, Cala Fornells (or Platjes de Fornells) is one of the best-planned of the newer developments, with imaginatively designed houses and villas, all different and set amid superb cactus gardens. It shares a beach with the odd-looking Cala Tirant across the water, a small growth of round white villas which is one of several Menorcan schemes that became stymied for one reason or another.

If you like geographical extremes, take the rough track to the most northerly point on the island, **Cap de Cavallería**. It's passable by car, with four farm gates to open and close, and leads past the site of the ancient Carthaginian and Roman port of Sanitja where nothing is to be seen today but a few small boats. At the tip of the narrow headland, walk along the cliff-top near the lighthouse for breathtaking views. The remains of gun emplacements date from the Spanish Civil War. Still further to the west, Binimel-la is another development that stopped almost before it started, but Menorcans favour its beach at weekends.

West from Mahón

You can do it slowly and make all the stops and side trips, or head straight for the other end of the island. The first way could take a day, a week or a month. The second, less than an hour. Adjust your plans to the time available, picking from the highlights that follow.

The busy main road from Mahón to Ciutadella at first runs parallel to the one built by order of the first British governor (now a delightfully quiet country lane named Ca-mí d'En Kane in his honour). Further west, today's road is superimposed on the old route. Near Mahón, you can begin with a feast of 3,000-year-old megalithic sites that will either satiate your appetite, or get you so excited that you'll go in search of more and more of them.

A few miles from Mahón, a sign to the left points down a lane to **Talatí de d'Alt.** Its elegantly slim *taula* has a "supporter" leaning against it, one of the stones that used to form a horseshoe-shaped enclosure and long ago fell into this position. Next to the *taula* you'll see the deep, dark columned room called a "hypostyle court" and, not far away, burial caves. It's a magical spot, especially in the quiet of the early morning or evening.

Back on the main road, a little further west, keep an eye open towards the fields on the north side. You're looking for two stone buildings shaped like the upturned boats, the *navetas* (prehistoric burial chambers) at **Rafal Rubí Nou**. That nearest to the road is in remarkable repair. You have to crawl in through the low doorway, but then you'll be surprised at the spacious interior, over 2 metres (7 ft.) high, with shelves at each end. See how few stones make the roof—or rather the ceiling, for this was a two-storey building, as you'll see if you climb on top. The other *naveta* is more of a ruin, but worth looking at for the beautifully recessed stone door frame, evidently designed to take a stone or wooden door.

South of the road, and most easily reached by the narrow lane from Alaior to Cala'n

Porter, **Torralba d'En Salort** has the most beautiful *taula* of all. There's no doubt, the ancients here had the art of stone construction down to a T. Climb the *talaiot* nearby to get an overview of the whole large site, and especially the way the *taula* was set in its horseshoe-shaped sanctuary. There has been some limited restoration here, including the re-erection of some smaller standing stones. Recent excavations and radiocarbon dating have put the *taula*'s date at about 900 B.C.

At the next crossroads to the south, in the direction of Cala'n Porter, turn west to reach a farm where the owner has painted red arrows to direct you to another remarkable site, **Torre Llisa Vell**—you'll make a dramatic entry into the *taula* precinct through the original doorway. Back on the Cala'n Porter road, head south for about half a kilometre and you'll see on your right the two massive *talaiots* of **Sonacasana**, where recent excavation has revealed a whole complex of buildings.

Alaior, white houses clustered on a low hill, looks at a distance almost like an Arab village. Though it's likely you'll pass through the outskirts several times on your

way around the island to some of the popular resorts, take the time to go to the top of the town and see its most attractive quarter. A long, sandy, gently sloping beach and sand dunes have brought obtrusive hotel and villa developments to the south coast at Sant Jaume and Son Bou, where besides waterslides and windsurfers, you can see the outline of a 5th-century basilica. It was discovered in 1951, right next to the beach at its eastern end.

A side-turning off the Alaior–Son Bou road is signposted to **Torre d'en Gaumés**, the biggest, most varied—and confusing—of the prehistoric settlements. Don't miss the hypostyle court, with its central supports and massive roof intact, or the water cisterns carved out like dungeons in the soft sandstone rock. (Don't fall in!) Shallow dishes cut in the flat stone are thought to have been used for settling debris out of the water before running it into the cisterns.

The south coast lacks the big inlets of the north, but it's rugged and cut by river valleys, so here, too, there is no road following the shore for any distance. Beach resorts may be almost adjoining, but if you want to drive from one to the other, it can mean a long detour back to the main road. To reach Sant Tomàs, a newish holiday complex on a narrow sandy beach backed by dunes, the road passes through a town whose chief claim on your attention is the battle over its name: San Cristóbal in Spanish, Es Migjorn Gran in *Menorquí*. Some signs to it have been painted over so often by enthusiasts for each language that a truce seems to have been declared, leaving them blank.

Choose a clear day if you can, and head for Mercadal halfway along the main east-west highway. Then climb the twisting but well-contoured road to the top of **Monte Toro**, Menorca's highest peak. It's only a modest 357 metres (1,171 ft.) high, but it stands up so sharply that it commands the best view of the whole island that you can get without flying.

Cala Santa Galdana is a horseshoe-shaped cove with white sand and turquoise water sheltered by cliffs and green pine woods. Too stunningly beautiful to resist, it has become one of Menorca's most popular holiday places. The main hotel is unfortunately obtrusive, but trees hide many of the other excesses of building. You'll escape some of the crowds by taking the half-hour's walk west along forest paths partly overgrown with broom to the pretty cove of **Macarella**. The even lovelier **Macarelleta** (a nudist beach) is ten more minutes' walk or a swim away. Both have been used from the earliest times: in places you'll be using pre-historic steps cut into the rock. (The two coves can also be reached from the west by car along rough unmarked tracks, if you can find them.)

A few miles to the west of Ferreríes, north of the cross-island road, walkers won't want to miss the climb to the hilltop ruins of the **castle of Santa Agueda.** The track forks right from a narrow lane heading north and climbs steeply. In places the path is only just passable on foot; then it may suddenly widen into a beauti-fully paved road before crumbling again. You'll be tempted to guess "Roman", and the experts would agree with you. Not much is left of the old castle, or the remote farm within the ramparts.

Ciutadella

"Little city", the name means, and until the early 18th century, it was the capital of Menorca. The British made the change: after all, they were on the island primarily because of Mahón's harbour, and Ciutadella's beau-tiful but narrow and shallow inlet could not compete.

The two cities are so unalike it's difficult to believe they are less than 45 kilometres (28 mi.) apart. You'll be hard put to find any Georgian windows in Ciutadella amidst the honey-coloured stone of baroque man-sions and palaces. But the dif-ference is essentially more one of atmosphere than of archi-tecture. Where Mahón means business, Ciutadella displays a gentler mood, remarkably un-affected by its summer visitors, merely putting up a few post-card stands and making room for more people in the bars and restaurants. There aren't many hotels—the resorts are out of town to the north and south.

Plaça Alfons III now marks the spot where the road from Mahón reached the old city gates. The gates have gone, but the cafés around the square probably began life by refresh-ing thirsty travellers. Stroll along the main street which bi-sects the old part of the city. It takes various different names but starts here as Carrer de Maó until it reaches Sa Plaça Nova. Then it becomes Carrer J.M. Quadrado, where one side, the lovely **Ses Voltes**, is com-pletely arcaded in Moorish style. Everywhere, shops and restaurants are ingeniously and discreetly fitted in: it's a perfect marriage of tradition and modern needs.

Don't hesitate to make diversions. There's so much wonderful stonework, its honey colour turning to gold as the sun goes down. Look especially for the carved doorway of **Església del Rosari** across from the cathedral down the little side street Carrer del Rosari. The **cathedral** itself, begun in the 13th century, is typically fortress-like and has been much modified over the centuries. The bishop's palace adjoins it— Ciutadella is still the ecclesiastical capital of the island.

Eventually you'll emerge from the main street into **Plaça d'es Born**, the ceremonial square on the heights above the harbour. Once the Moors' parade ground, it's lined with imposing buildings: the former Ajuntament (now the police headquarters) and great 19th-century mansions in the course of restoration. The obelisk in the middle of the square commemorates a brave defence against 15,000 besieging Turks in 1558. The town fell after nine days, and the survivors were carried off into slavery.

Steps and a ramp lead down to the **port**, where a long curving inlet is lined with fishing boats large and small on one side, pleasure craft segregated on the other and—sign of increasing tourism—a glass-bottomed boat or two. Morning and evening you can watch the fishermen return with varied catches to be met by their womenfolk. A lot of the fish goes only a few yards, to restaurants on the waterfront, some housed in caverns in the base of the harbour bastion, and expanding onto the quay on warm nights. Bars and discos, too, make this area the focus of Ciutadella nightlife.

It may seem strange to find a statue of the American Civil War hero, Admiral David Farragut, on the southern edge of town near the second, smaller inlet. His father was born on the island and emigrated to the United States. The first admiral of the U.S. Navy was declared an honorary Menorcan and came to pay a visit in 1867.

Prehistory near Ciutadella

Five kilometres (3 mi.) from the city, just south of the main road, stands the **Naveta d'es Tudons**, not to be missed. A burial chamber claimed to be

Fairground figure at Ciutadella doesn't scare this curious visitor.

the oldest roofed building in Europe, it dates from around 1000 B.C. As you'll see when you crawl in through the tiny entrance, it's a double-decker, with a small anteroom where you can stand upright and enter either floor. When it was excavated in the 1950s and again in the '70s, many bones were found, and some bronze ornaments. Restoration work done at the same time accounts for the pristine condition. Overall, it's 14 metres (46 ft.) long, about 6.5 metres (21 ft.) wide and up to 4 metres (13 ft.) high. Notice the massive slabs that form the twin roofs: not having devised the true arch, this was one way the ancients could use stone to make a large room.

If you've developed a taste for *taulas,* two intriguing sites are hidden not far away. Heading away from Ciutadella, just beyond Naveta d'es Tudons take the next lane to the south, and after 2.5 kilometres (1.5 mi.) turn left down a farm track to Torre Trencada. A signpost then points across the fields to the *taula* and a huge cave. Back on the main road, the next turning south, through stone gateposts (close the gates!) and across a farmyard, brings you to the mysterious, largely unexcavated **Torre 78 Llafuda,** almost concealed by

trees. There's a wonderful view from the *talaiot* of the strange countryside around.

Head out of Ciutadella on the road towards Sant Joan de Missa and branch towards Son Saura, and after 6 kilometres (4 mi.) you'll come to the prehistoric walled town of **Son Catlar**, situated in the farmland to the east of the road. Ask the farmer politely if you may look around, and he'll equally politely invite you to go ahead. You can walk round the 900-metre-long (2,880-ft.) walls, which possibly date from about 600 B.C., though on the southeastern side you'll see places where, much later, the Romans built bastions. The *taula* seems to have been deliberately broken off—possibly the Romans turned the precinct into a temple.

North of Ciutadella, on the road to Punta Nati, turn right at the old car dump to reach the *talaiots* of **Torre Vella**. The most northerly is unusual in having its entrance and a large interior room intact.

Beaches and Resorts near Ciutadella

Almost every accessible cove and inlet on the coast near Ciutadella has been developed in a rash of *urbanizaciónes*. This has created a lot of holiday homes, hotels and associated facilities, but the effect can be rather dull and suburban. Beaches are very small, which makes them overcrowded in high summer, but many of the developments are in the form of villa complexes with their own communal pools.

South of the city, Santandria's narrow sandy beach can be dirty. Most of the coastline consists of sharp rocks, but when you find a spot to swim out from, the clear water is enticing and perfect for snorkelling. Cala Blanca with its huge white hotel and apartments can be especially crowded—or lively, to look on the bright side. The windswept south-western corner of the island, Cap d'Artrutx, has been heavily built up, but fortunately the rules have kept construction back 100 metres or so from the sea. East of the cape, Cala en Bosc has a sheltered harbour, with an attractive marina cut out behind the coast, and good sports facilities.

Further to the east, the sea is reached only by narrow lanes and farm tracks, but local people and regular visitors reckon it worthwhile to get away from the crowds. Sometimes so many head for the remote spots, they create a crowd there too. Cala Turqueta is one of their favourites, reached from Ciutadella by the Sant Joan de Missa road. Another, Son Saura, down the lane past Son Catlar, entails the opening and closing of no fewer than eight farm gates along a potholed dirt track. It's a chance to see rural Menorca, but since the beach can be covered with heaps of dry weed, you may not think it worth the effort.

Just west of Ciutadella, Cala Blanes and the vast area of villas and hotels near Cala Forcat make a self-contained holiday town, but their two often scruffy little beaches can hardly cope with the summer influx. The north-west corner of the island, in contrast, has scarcely been touched by tourism, and anxious environmentalists want it declared a no-go area for development. Some building has already jumped the gun at **Cala Morell**, where little white houses and blocks of villas have sprouted on the east side of one of the loveliest bays on the north coast. A maze of paths leads down to the rocky shore and around the cliffs, a geology textbook of tortured strata. Notice the weird aggregate—a sort of natural concrete composed of different rocks. You'll be tempted to swim from the ledges here, but beware of treading on spiny sea urchins. **79**

What to Do

Sports and Other Activities

To get in, on or under the water is the aim of most summer visitors, and both Mallorca and Menorca can offer just about every known method. The mild climate means a longer season for sports ashore, with a mass of other diversions and some special attractions that children will enjoy as a break from the beach.

Swimming

Gently sloping expanses of sand, rocks to dive off into deep water, sheltered bay or open sea: the choice is enormous, so try to find out what the beach is like before you choose your resort. For learning to windsurf (boardsail), pick somewhere with plenty of shallow water (such as Ses Salines on Menorca). That will suit the small children in your party, too, but keep an eye on them just the same in the summer crowds. Lifeguards are rare, though larger beaches do have first-aid stations. A few more words of warning: beware of spiky sea urchins when swimming off rocks; and remember the sun is still burning you when you're in the water, even though you may feel cool. In California, where trends begin, they're still sun-worshipping—but covered with protective creams up to Factor 28.

When the beach or pool begins to pall, make a bigger splash on a giant waterslide. **Aquatic parks** at S'Arenal (with a reptile house, too) and Magalluf claim to be the best and the biggest in Europe. Others are at Alcúdia and Binissalem (with a wax museum), and at Sant Jaume on Menorca. The staff are safety-conscious, so parents can relax at the parks' pools and cafés while offspring scream down the corkscrews and roller-coasters. The larger parks are quite expensive, so plan to stay awhile to get your money's worth.

Boating and Sailing

Escape the crowds and sail to an idyllic deserted cove. That's the object of thousands who keep their own boats here all year round—countless harbours and marinas create a forest of masts. You can get away

Too late to turn back now on this giant waterslide at Magalluf! No lack of amusements at the big, brash resort.

from it all, too, by hiring various sorts of craft for an hour, day or week, at many beaches and hotels. The stately "pedalo" for two won't go fast, but it's stable enough for adults to take along small children. Sailing dinghies are widely available, with lessons for complete novices to get them started. There are windsurfing (boardsailing) schools, too, and you can find boards to hire and conditions to suit everyone, from nervous be ginners to acrobatic experts.

Someone else will do the work if you take an **excursion**. Boats link all the resorts fringing the Bay of Palma, from S'Arenal to Portals Vells; you can use them like a bus service. From Port de Pollença or Port d'Alcúdia, cruise round the cliffs of Cap de Formentor. Sailings from Port de Sóller are the way to see the rugged northwest coast. Trips from Colònia de Sant Jordi/Campos let you land on the strange isle of Cabrera (see p. 55). Enquire about schedules for summer links between Port d'Alcúdia and Ciutadella, Menorca. On Menorca, take a cruise round the historic harbour of Mahón (Maó) or go by water to the loveliest beaches, instead of bumping by car down unmarked and stony tracks.

Snorkelling and Diving

Take your mask and flippers—the water is crystal clear, especially off rocks and away from near-landlocked harbours. To spear-fish you need a licence, and can only do it 200 metres (650 ft.) or more away from beaches. Scuba-diving equipment is for hire, if you have a qualification from your home country. To gain this diploma during your holiday, take a five-day series of lessons, usually starting in a hotel pool and graduating to supervised dives to a depth of 12 metres (39 ft.).

Water-skiing

An expensive business, this, especially if you're taking lessons and not progressing too well. Try to negotiate a big discount if you intend to water-ski a lot. Designation of areas for different water sports is not always enforced or clear, so expect to find swimmers and craft in your way. Conversely, if you are swimming, try to make yourself obvious, and keep out of areas where power-boats and jet-skis are operating.

Fishing

Locals and visitors alike fish from rocky shores and harbour jetties. Experts say there's a greater chance of making a catch in the cooler days of spring and autumn, and that the hours after sunset are better for taking the real prizes, such as tuna. To fish from a boat, obtain a licence from the Comandancia de Marina, Moll Vell 1, Palma, and for freshwater fishing in the reservoirs, a permit from I.C.O.N.A., Passatge de Guillermo de Torrela, 1, Palma.

Golf

A handful of courses near Palma and several 9-hole courses near the east coast are varied and challenging enough for the best players. At most of them, you can hire equipment and take lessons. Beautifully landscaped Son Vida hosts the Balearics' Open, and Santa

Ponça claims one of Europe's longest holes, the 590-metre (645-yd.) 10th. Plan to tee off early: at times, you'll spend a lot of time waiting for players ahead of you. Menorca has a 9-hole course at Son Parc on the north coast, and another in the south-east. For further information, contact the Federación Balear de Golf, Avinguda del Rei Jaume III, 17, Palma.

Walking

Pure pleasure, it's literally the only way to go if you want to reach some of the hilltop castles and remoter stretches of coast. April and May are reckoned to be the best months, when a wild profusion of flowers will put a spring in your step. In the hotter months, start early or make use of the long evenings. On Mallorca the mountains of the north-west make for the most dramatic scenery, as on the climb to Castell d'Alaró (see p. 44) or between the Monastery of Lluc and the coast. Reserve a Saturday to walk to the Castell del Rei near Pollença (see p. 48). On Menorca, search for more elusive prehistoric sites, take the cliff paths of the north-west or south coasts, and climb to Santa Agueda (see p. 75). The Balearic Government Tourist Office, Avinguda del Rei Jaume III, 10, Palma, publishes a leaflet describing other good walks. Wear sturdy rubber-soled shoes for climbing over rocks.

Cycling

In the spring, serious cyclists come in their thousands to Mallorca from all over Europe, bringing their expensive machines with them. Colourful groups tear all over the island in races and time-trials or grind up the steepest mountain passes just for the fun of it. As they leave, summer tourists take over, making gentler progress on the bikes they've hired at the resorts. It's a wonderful way to get around. If you're going to join in, check the brakes and tyres and make sure a strong lock is included.

Bird-watching

The resident birds would be enticing enough, but it's the visitors that generate most excitement. Migrants from Africa stop to rest in the Balearics, and some stay for the summer. Birds of prey rare elsewhere in Europe are spotted here, and stretches of water (S'Albufera and Salines de Llevant on Mallorca, and S'Albufera on Menorca) attract waterfowl.

Hunting and Shooting

A very popular island sport; hunters bag hare, rabbit, duck, quail and partridge. For details about hunting permits, check with local or foreign tourist offices or write to the Federación Balear de Caza, Carrer Reial, 6, Local 16, Palma.

More Sports and Games

Many hotels and villa or apartment complexes have their own **tennis** courts, and **squash** is slowly spreading. Despite the increased facilities, you often have to book a day ahead. You pay by the hour, and may be able to hire rackets or take lessons at the bigger resorts and clubs.

There are ranches and stables scattered over both islands where you can hire a mount and go off **horseback-riding.** Magalluf and Ca'n Picafort have circuits for **go-karting.** You can try **micro-light flying** from fields near Cap Blanc and Campos, or follow the local dare-devils by **hang-gliding** from mountaintops.

If you want something gentler, you'll probably find fellow **bridge** players in the big holiday hotels, especially out of high season. The same places usually have **pool** and **table-tennis** facilities.

Just Watching

This is Spain, so you'll expect **bullfights**. They're staged on summer Sunday afternoons in Palma's big bullring (Plaça de Toros), and less regularly at Inca and Muro. (Menorca has no bullfights.) If you've never seen the *corrida,* perhaps you should. Whatever your reaction, you'll be witnessing an ancient ritual and may come to understand why *aficionados* regard it as an art form. Choose your seat carefully: *sol* means you'll be in the full heat and dazzle of the sun, at least at first. The more expensive *sombra* means shade, and *sol y sombra* means, logically, some of each, though the sun won't be in your eyes.

Less controversially beautiful, **trotting races** are held every Sunday, all year round, at the tracks *(Hipodròm)* at Son Pardo near Palma and Manacor, and near Mahón and Ciutadella. The informal atmosphere and casual-looking handicap starts can be deceptive. Competition is fierce, with foreign owners and horses involved. Betting is through a centralized "tote" system.

If you fancy your chances of picking winning **greyhounds**, head for Palma's *Canodròm,* Camí de Jesús, where they run several times a week.

Not Only for Children

Parrots show an aptitude for counting, sea lions for balancing balls and dolphins for having fun doing amazing tricks. It all happens several times a day at **Marineland**, west of Palma at Costa d'En Blanes.

Opposite the Aquapark at Magalluf, El Dorado is a complete town straight out of cowboy films, and the convincing setting for a **Wild West** show. Stunt men stage saloon-bar punch-ups and fall off horses, and Red Indians ride full tilt down Main Street. After spaghetti western shoot-outs, you can eat real spaghetti or barbecued steaks in the town's real restaurants.

La Granja near Esporles (see p. 39–40) is a beautiful old country estate with craftspeople at work and folk dance displays.

Rhinos, antelopes and ostriches live happily in the Reserva Africana (see p. 51), a small **Safari Park** near Cala Millor. You can drive through as slowly as you like or ride on an open waggon.

Everyone loves the old-style **trains** running between Palma and Sóller (see p. 43). Mallorca's other line, from Palma to Inca, is not so picturesque, but think about it if you plan to visit **86** Inca's Thursday market.

Shopping

Shopping Hours

Most stores are open from 9 a.m. to 1 or 1.30 p.m. and again from 4.30 or 5 to 8 p.m. The hours in between are devoted to lunch and the siesta. The big department stores and hypermarkets of Palma deny tradition by staying open all the day. In summer, shops in the resorts may stay open until 10 p.m. Practically everywhere closes on Sundays.

Best Buys

Mallorca and Menorca alike are celebrated for their **leather**: famous makes of shoes sold in Paris or Italy are quite likely to have come from the islands. So does some of the finest leather and suede clothing, much of it from factories in Inca, which you can visit. You're even more welcome in the factory retail outlets there, and at Ciutadella and Alaior on Menorca. Although the signs say "factory prices", these may not be much lower than in the stores of Palma—a lot of the products on sale won't have come from that factory anyway. They should, however, be significantly less than in your home country, or even in mainland Spain.

While you admire the quality

of the very best leather—it can seem as supple as silk—do check for flaws and look at the stitching. Some of the items are "seconds": that may be why they are here. You may be able to negotiate discounts.

Mallorcan **artificial pearls**, manufactured in Manacor (see pp. 58–59), are exported in huge numbers. They're a good buy and prices don't vary much from shop to shop. There may be a small saving at the factory showroom, and it's here you'll have the biggest choice.

Wines and many other **alcoholic drinks** are still cheap by the standards of the rest of Europe. This applies especially to foreign brands made under licence in Spain. Cuban **cigars** are priced at less than you would pay elsewhere in western Europe.

Souvenirs

A few "souvenir supermarkets" on the main roads, near some of the tourist attractions of Mallorca, will give you an idea of the range available. Everything "Spanish" that was ever devised for the tourist trade is piled high, from charming craftwork to laughable junk. But don't assume that you will find the best prices in these places. They are intended to cater for excursion parties.

Smaller tourist-oriented shops aren't likely to offer the best prices either. Check prices and look elsewhere as well, including in street markets. **Embroidered linen** can be attractive. So can handmade **baskets** (though some come from China) and **glass** items. Authentically Mallorcan are the weird pottery figures called *siurells*. Painted in red and green on white, something similar has been around since Phoenician times. They have a spout-like whistle, and rather phallic versions are not just a modern joke: fertility is part of the *siurell* lore.

Shopping Tips

Palma overshadows everywhere else on Mallorca in the scale and sophistication of its shops. Other towns scarcely try to compete, so it's to the capital you'll have to go if you want a wide choice. Some of the most fashionable shops are on Avinguda del Rei Jaume III. Look on Carrer Plateria for jewellery, and Carrer Jaume II for clothing and fans. Plaça Major holds a craft market on Fridays and Saturdays. On Menorca, both Mahón and Ciutadella have smaller but attractive pedestrianized shopping areas.

Ask for a discount if you're

paying cash, or even if you aren't. But don't expect to bargain, except discreetly in the antique shops, and in open-air markets. The value-added tax (IVA) imposed on most goods can be refunded on major purchases if you are exporting them. To obtain the rebate, you fill in a form provided by the shop. One copy is kept by the shop; the other three must be presented at customs on your departure, with the goods. The rebate will be forwarded to you at your home address.

Market Days

The same sellers move with their goods from town to town, so markets don't vary much. All but the smallest places have one, on the same day each week and usually in the morning (as shown below, except where marked "p.m.").

Sunday: Alcúdia, Felanitx, Muro, Pollença, Santa María.

Monday: Calvia, Manacor.

Tuesday: Artà, Ca'n Picafort (p.m.), Mahón.

Wednesday: Andratx, Port de Pollença, Sineu.

Thursday: Alaior, Campos, Inca, S'Arenal.

Friday: Algaida, Binissalem, Son Servera.

Saturday: Bunyola, Cala Ratjada, Ciutadella, Palma, Sóller.

Entertainment

The bigger the resort, the more varied the activities. There's something for everyone.

Discos, of course—you'll probably be offered tickets while you're lying on the beach, even free ones if the owners are trying to boost a place, or if the *tiquetero* thinks your good looks will be an asset. **Bars** galore: local, Scandinavian, German, French and British décors, accents and beers, huge or intimate, meals, snacks or nothing to eat, pool tables or dance floors, loud music or loud TVs.

Films are usually shown dubbed into Spanish, with rare exceptions in the biggest resorts. Islanders have taken to video rental, and though most stocks are naturally in Spanish, there are some in English where the foreign population is concentrated.

Bigger package hotels boast entertainers operating in two or three languages to ginger up the older crowd in competitions, sing-songs and a more sedate sort of dancing.

Hand-in-hand with the revival of the island languages has come renewed interest in Balearic culture. Children learn the traditional dances, and shows are put on by **folk dance** troupes at the resorts as well as during fiestas. The oldest dances, survivals from Moorish times, are usually performed in the mountain villages: in *els cossiers,* groups move together to the rhythm of drums and the sound of tambourine and shawm (an ancient form of oboe). Another dance, the *parado,* resembles a courtly minuet: it's performed in Valldemossa in the square beside the monastery. Menorca's distinctive dances include the *ball d'es cossil,* thought to be derived from Scottish dancing. Something like the English may-pole dance, it's performed at the fiesta in Es Migjorn Gran.

Hotels sometimes organize **flamenco** nights; even though these songs and dances come from Andalusia, they've become a feature of holidays in other parts of Spain. The shows are more or less authentic, with singers, dancers and guitarists, though they tend to stick to the more cheerful *cante chico* (light song) rather than the slow, sobbingly emotional *cante jondo* (song of the soul). Amateur attempts by audience members hauled on stage are hardly likely to be authentic.

The **dinner-and-show excursions** widely offered include more flamenco, cabaret and striptease. At the Casino de Mallorca, depending on the package you opt for, you'll get dinner, house wines and entry into the gaming rooms (you'll need your passport) to test your luck at roulette, blackjack, craps and slot machines—or just watch. The show typically doesn't finish until the small hours, so be sure to take a siesta beforehand.

Medieval nights hosted by a wicked count, pirates, barbecues with folk dancing; there's something different every night if you have the stamina.

Festivals *(Fiestas)*

Saints' days and holidays are so frequent that the chances are good that at least one will coincide with your stay.

Jan 5	Procession of the Magi, Palma. The Three Kings arrive by boat, amid noisy rejoicing, and give out presents in Plaça Cort.
Jan 17	Sant Antoní, patron of animals. Bonfires and dances, processions on foot and horseback in Palma and inland towns. Climbing the stripped pine tree at Pollença.

Mar or Apr	Holy Week processions in most towns. In Palma, men carry holy images to the sound of muffled drums.
May **(2nd week)**	Sóller celebrates a great victory over pirate raiders in 1561.
June 23–24	Sant Joan (St. John). Fiesta in Muro and Ciutadella; parade of decorated horses through narrow streets, riders perform daring equestrian feats.
June 29	Sant Petro, patron of fishermen. Procession of boats at Port d'Alcúdia.
July 15–16	Virgen del Carme. Processions of decorated boats at fishing ports (Port d'Andratx by day, Cala Ratjada and Port de Sóller by night).
July 24–26	Sant Jaume (St. James). Many fiestas, e.g. Es Castell (Villacarlos), bullfights at Palma, Inca, Muro, devil-dances at Algaida.
July 28	Santa Catalina Thomàs. Procession of decorated carts in Valldemossa, and concert in monastery.
July 30	Inca Festival. Bullfights.
Aug 2	Pollença stages a mock battle between Moors and Christians.
Aug	International Festival of Music, Palma, including concerts in the wonderful cloisters of Sant Francesc.
Aug 10–12	Sant Llorenc. At Alaior, Song Festival and dramatic equestrian events.
Aug 25–27	Sant Lluis. Fiesta and parade in honour of the name saint of this Menorcan town.
Sept 8	Nativity of the Virgin. Processions, folk events in many places.
Sept–Oct	Binissalem Wine Festival, with bagpipers, fireworks, dancing and, of course, winetasting.
Oct 31	All Saints' Day (Halloween). Necklaces of special sweets are given to children. Dances and parties.
Nov **(1st Thursday)**	Dijous Bo or "Good Thursday". Agricultural fair at Inca, folk music and dances.
Dec 31	Palma celebrates the anniversary of its recapture from the Moors in 1229. Processions, dances.

Eating Out

In the Balearics you could live entirely on "fast food" or Italian, German or English cuisine at beach cafés and resort restaurants. Many hotels seem to be convinced—probably from past experience—that a bland international diet, rather than indigenous dishes, is what visitors want. They frequently serve up "buffets" of various salads and hot and cold dishes, the same you've always eaten at home. As a gesture towards "Spanishness", *paella* is widely offered, and although this combination of saffron rice with permutations of seafoods, onion, garlic, pork, rabbit, peppers, peas, etc. can be delicious, it's a traditional lunch dish from Valencia, not the islands. *Gazpacho*, the cold and zesty "liquid salad" soup, is another import, coming from Andalusia.

Fortunately, there's a different world awaiting. To enter it, you have only to find out where—and what—the islanders themselves like to eat. Where? Try the villages, including the ones near Palma, and the inland towns (Inca is well known for its restaurants). Look for unpretentious places and half-hidden cellars. What? Read on.

Local Specialities

There's a wonderful variety of dishes to sample, stemming from the different influences that came in waves to the Balearics. But remember that for centuries, people here were poor. Their history is reflected in simple robust peasant fare made from the healthiest ingredients. It can be filling—that was the intention—and helpings tend to be enormous (some places will serve half-portions [*media-ración*]).

Pa amb oli, literally bread with oil, has evolved into a range of open sandwiches. Country bread is spread with a little olive oil, perhaps rubbed with sun-dried tomatoes and topped with olives or capers. Today's more opulent versions are loaded with cheese or some of the excellent local ham.

Sopas Mallorquínas—in the plural form, as shown on menus—is something between a soup and a stew, a combination of vegetables (cauliflower, onion, whatever's in season), olives and a little garlic, presented with slices of bread to soak up the juices. Fancier versions may include pork and

From garlic to bunyelos: treats at a roadside stall in Vilafranca de Bonany.

mushrooms too. They're all served in an earthenware platter, or *greixonera de terra,* which in turn gave its name to a whole range of stews: *greixonera de peix,* a fish stew, and *greixonera d'aubergínies* (*berenjenas* in Castilian), a mouth-watering preparation of aubergines (eggplant).

The islanders' liking for a "fry-up" wasn't acquired from the British. Given the easy availability of olive oil, it was only natural to use it to sauté whatever came to hand. *Tumbet* is a combination of peppers, aubergines, tomatoes and potatoes cooked in oil, and *frit Mallorquí,* a tasty concoction of strips of fried liver, kidney, peppers, leeks and other optional extras.

In the old days, self-sufficiency was the watchword. The habit dies hard, and after rain you'll still see people out at night carrying lights. They're looking for snails, *caracoles,* which turn up on many menus, served with a garlic mayonnaise. Another one-time abundant free supply of protein, rabbit (*conejo*), appears in traditional stews. Especially on Mallorca, every rural family kept pigs, and many still do. So pork and all its by-products are a mainstay, including hams and bacons, *botifarró* (a spicy blood sausage) and *lechona asada,* roast sucking pig, which is really a Christmas dish but features year-round on menus.

Mallorca's justly famous *sobrasada,* a sausage made from pork and red peppers (the mild variety) is something of an acquired taste. Try some: you may love it, even eaten with honey, in the local fashion. The combining of sweet and savoury flavours, and putting almonds in stews, may date from the time of the Moors (although they would not have eaten pork, of course). *Zarzuela de mariscos,* for example, contains shellfish, tomatoes, garlic, wine and almonds. Look out for seasonal savoury pies, some being the speciality of just one town; *espinagada* is an eel-and-spinach pie, *panades de peix* are fish pies.

Crème caramel (*flan*) is as curiously universal on the Balearics as the mainland, but you ought to be able to find some sweet pastries and pies or some of the almond and honey desserts that are a legacy of the Moors.

As you drive through inland towns (such as Vilafranca de Bonany) in the late afternoon, watch out for women seated at their front doors selling *bunyelos.* They're bite-sized round doughnuts, deep-fried in lard and dipped in sugar. Who knows, Mallorcans may have invented the doughnut. After all, some of them claim Christopher Columbus.

Island Differences

Although many dishes are common to both isles, don't be surprised to find big variations between Mallorca and Menorca. Their distinctive histories and the smaller island's colder, windier winters led to differences in crops and customs. Menorcan cooks use more cream, butter and cheese, and correspondingly less olive oil, though they do make a simple soup called *oliaigua*, "oil and water" (it contains eggs too!).

Vestiges of English in the *Menorquí* language hint at words introduced during the periods of British rule—*púdins, píquels* and *grevi*—but it's a French word that has carried Menorca around the gastronomic world. A running battle continues over the exact origin, but there's little doubt that *mayonnaise* is named after Mahón. One story has it that the sauce was concocted in Paris, and named in honour of the French victory of 1756 over the English. Menorcans will have none of that: they believe it's a local invention, made famous when it was served to the Duc de Richelieu during the French occupation.

Fish

People coming to islands naturally expect to eat plenty of fish. Here, they still can, but at a price. Stocks in the Mediterranean are depleted and the local fishermen cannot keep up with the demand, especially in summer. Supplies have to be brought from Spain's Atlantic ports, and they're expensive, or frozen (and sometimes unfortunately both). *Salmonete* is red mullet, which *is* caught locally. So are some of the *langostas,* spiny lobsters found on many a menu and a big attraction in the fish restaurants of Fornells on the north coast of Menorca. *Caldereta de langosta* is a delicious lobster stew. *Merluza,* a Spanish standby, is hake, and *bacalao* is cod, usually salted and dried and not suited to every taste. Farmed trout (*trucha*) and sole (*lenguado*), brought in frozen, feature on many cheaper menus.

Restaurants and "Menús"

Spanish restaurants are officially graded by one to five forks, the latter being the most elegant. But forks are awarded for facilities and menu size, which may have little to do with the quality of the food.

Many offer a *menú del día,* a daily set menu. (If you ask for the "menu", the waiter will **95** probably think the set meal is what you mean. If you actually want to look at the full list of dishes available, ask for *la carta* or *la lista de platos*.) For a fixed price, you'll get three courses: soup or salad, main dish (with a small choice) and dessert (ice-cream, a piece of fruit or pastry), plus wine, beer or bottled water. Typically, the cost is about one-third of what you'd pay if you ordered from the regular menu. Many restaurants only have a *menú del día* at lunchtime, but if you are on a budget, don't be reluctant to ask if there is one, anywhere, any time. No place worth its salt should make you feel uncomfortable for choosing their "day's special".

Incidentally, most prices include service, but it's customary to leave something extra.

Rest your feet and watch the passing show: the terrace café is a way of life.

Bars and Cafés

These establishments are an important institution in Spanish life. Some open at first light to cater for early-morning workers; nearly all are open by 8.30 a.m. to serve breakfast. Open-air cafés are justifiably popular with tourists. One of the great pleasures of the Mediterranean is to sit outside in the early morning with a *café con leche* (white coffee) and watch a town come to life. The price of a coffee buys you a seat at a table for as long as you care to sit there.

While in a café or bar you might be approached by lottery-ticket vendors, flower-sellers and bootblacks. If you don't want what they offer, simply say *no, gracias.*

Wines and spirits are served at all hours in bars and cafés. It's usually 10 to 15 per cent cheaper to take a drink at the bar rather than at a table.

The days are sadly gone when you were given a free bite of food with your drink in a bar, but the word for these morsels survives. *Tapa* means "lid", from the little plate that covered the glass and carried the snack. Some bars specialize in *tapas,* featuring a line of dishes, hot and cold, for you to pick from. Portions are larger now that you're paying for them: per-haps five different choices can substitute for a conventional main course.

You don't need to know the tapa names, you can just point. It's a great way of making new discoveries among a range that might run from meat balls to potato salad, tripe, eels or stewed baby octopuses. Look out for *boquerones,* anchovies freshly prepared, not tinned, in vinegar, oil and garlic, and, most common of all on *tapa* counters, the *tortilla* of eggs, potatoes and onions, fried until golden in olive oil.

Mealtimes

The locals eat just a little earlier on the islands than people on the mainland. Breakfast may start at 7.30 a.m. and go on until 10. Lunch runs typically from 1 to 3 p.m. and dinner begins around 8.30 p.m., although some people will drift in as late as 10.30 p.m.

Concessions have been made to impatient tourists, however, and hotels may start breakfast at 7 a.m., lunch at 12.30 p.m. and dinner as outrageously early as 7 p.m.

Breakfast

The Spanish make a point of treating breakfast as unimportant. The islanders are no great exception, despite having their **97** very own delicious *ensaimada,* a floatingly light round bun, presented as a spiral of dough sprinkled with icing sugar. Augmented with cream, almonds or pumpkin jam, it makes a sinful snack at any time, but try it for breakast with coffee on a sunny terrace. Go ahead, dunk it—you may start a habit you'll find hard to kick. At Palma airport, you'll see addicts taking home special flat boxes up to a yard across containing *ensaimadas.*

Hotels seem to write their own rules, and breakfasts range from vast buffets included in the room rate to a bread roll and tasteless coffee for which you have to pay extra. If the latter's the case, head out to a bar or cafeteria, where you will be sure of great coffee. Some of them offer an "English breakfast" of bacon and eggs, too.

Drinks

No question about it, the islands truly are a drinker's paradise. Superb fresh fruit juices abound. Try some of the novel thirst-quenching mixtures such as peach-and-grape. The local beer is fairly cheap, good and served cold, but if you want the one you always have in the pub at home, it's probably here too. In the bigger resorts, there is a staggering (the word is only too appropriate at times) variety of British, German, Dutch and other draught and bottled brands at about twice the domestic price.

Mallorca produces wines in various lowland areas and sheltered spots, particularly around Binissalem, and it's interesting to try them—they may not be very distinguished (the firm Jaume Mesquida is considered by some to produce the best) but they're better than the inferior bulk wines that some restaurants serve as house wines. Ordering the house wine (*vino de la casa*) is a useful economy measure—and many Spanish diners do it without a second thought—but some of it is dreadful. Ask what it is, and whether you can have a taste. If you favour something better, try some of the much-improved Catalan wines (Penedés produces the best) or the Riojas, white or red.

Spanish sparkling wines can be cheap and mass-produced. The word *cava* tends to be applied indiscriminately, but it theoretically should be reserved for the better bubbly produced by the same method as champagne. Some can be sweeter than you're used to; if you really want it dry, look for *brut* (even *seco*, "dry", may not be such).

Sangría is a favourite summer wine and fruit mixture—every bar has its own recipe. Beware, it's so cool and smooth that you don't realize the kick it can have.

To many, Spain means sherry *(jerez)*, and every kind is here. Pale, dry *fino* is sometimes drunk not only as an apéritif but with soup and fish courses. Rich dark *oloroso* goes well after dinner. Spanish brandy can be excellent or rough: you mostly get what you pay for. Gin has been made in Menorca since the British Navy was there, and several brands come from the mainland, too. Other spirits are made under licence in Spain, and are often a lot cheaper than imported Scotch whisky, for example. There are "lookalikes" as well, which imitate the labels of well-known brands. Hitting below the belt, some bars may refill famous-name bottles with something that ought to be a lot cheaper.

Finally, to round off a meal, try one of the locally made liqueurs, either aromatic *hierbas seca* ("dry herbs"), *hierbas dulce* ("sweet herbs") or sticky *palo*, made from carob seeds.

To Help You Order...

The local dialects are gaining ground on Mallorca and Menorca, but Castilian Spanish is still the lingua franca for tourists, and useful in the restaurant.

Could we have a table? **¿Nos puede dar una mesa?**
Do you have a set menu? **¿Tiene un menú del día?**
I'd like a/an/some... **Quisiera...**

beer	una cerveza	**milk**	leche
bread	pan	**mineral water**	agua mineral
coffee	un café	**napkin**	una servilleta
condiments	los condimentos	**potatoes**	patatas
cutlery	los cubiertos	**rice**	arroz
dessert	un postre	**salad**	una ensalada
fish	pescado	**sandwich**	un bocadillo
fruit	fruta	**soup**	una sopa
glass	un vaso	**sugar**	azúcar
ice-cream	un helado	**tea**	un té
meat	carne	**(iced) water**	agua (fresca)
menu	la carta	**wine**	vino

... And Read the Menu

Spanish	English	Spanish	English
aceitunas	**olives**	guisantes	**peas**
ajo	**garlic**	helado	**ice-cream**
albaricoques	**apricots**	higos	**figs**
albóndigas	**meatballs**	huevos	**eggs**
almejas	**baby clams**	jamón	**ham**
anchoas	**anchovies**	judías	**beans**
anguila	**eel**	langosta	**spiny lobster**
arroz	**rice**	langostino	**prawn**
asado	**roast**	lenguado	**sole**
atún	**tunny (tuna)**	limón	**lemon**
bacalao	**codfish**	lomo	**loin**
besugo	**sea bream**	manzana	**apple**
bistec	**beef steak**	mariscos	**shellfish**
boquerones	**fresh anchovies**	mejillones	**mussels**
caballa	**mackerel**	melocotón	**peach**
calamares	**squid**	merluza	**hake**
(a la romana)	**(deep fried)**	naranja	**orange**
callos	**tripe**	ostras	**oysters**
cangrejo	**crab**	pastel	**cake**
caracoles	**snails**	pescado	**fish**
cebollas	**onions**	pescadilla	**whiting**
cerdo	**pork**	pez espada	**swordfish**
champiñones	**mushrooms**	pimiento	**green pepper**
chorizo	**a spicy pork sausage**	piña	**pineapple**
		plátano	**banana**
chuleta	**chops**	pollo	**chicken**
cordero	**lamb**	postre	**dessert**
dorada	**sea-bass**	pulpitos	**baby octopus**
ensalada	**salad**	queso	**cheese**
entremeses	**hors-d'oeuvre**	salchichón	**salami**
estofado	**stew**	salmonete	**red mullet**
filete	**fillet**	salsa	**sauce**
flan	**caramel mould**	sandía	**watermelon**
frambuesas	**raspberries**	sopa	**soup**
fresas	**strawberries**	ternera	**veal**
frito	**fried**	tortilla	**omelette**
galletas	**biscuits (cookies)**	tostada	**toast**
		trucha	**trout**
gambas	**shrimp**	uvas	**grapes**
granadas	**pomegranates**	verduras	**vegetables**

BLUEPRINT for a Perfect Trip

How to Get There

BY AIR

Scheduled flights

Palma de Mallorca's airport (see p. 106) is linked by daily non-stop flights to London and Frankfurt, with frequent flights to many other European cities, either non-stop or via Madrid or Barcelona. The number increases greatly in the high (summer) season. There are also some non-stop flights from London (Luton or Gatwick airports) to Menorca in summer. For intercontinental air travellers, the usual gateways to Spain

are the Madrid and Barcelona airports, which have several daily connections to both Palma and Mahón (Maó), Menorca.

The flight time from London to Palma or Mahón is just over 2 hours, from New York to Barcelona, approximately 8 hours. Apart from standard fares there are numerous money-saving options, depending on when you book and how long you stay.

Charter Flights and Package Tours

From the U.K. and Eire: An enormous choice is available from major tour operators and from many smaller and specialist companies. You may find there's a charter flight from an airport close to your home. Good travel agents can assist you in selecting the most suitable combination of destination and accommodation. Prices vary dramatically with the season, hotel (or villa/apartment) category and the time between booking and departure. Extraordinary bargains may be on offer if you can travel at short notice, both for "flight only" tickets and for packages that include accommodation.

From North America: Most charter flights operate to Madrid or the Costa del Sol, and may be combined with Mallorca in a package. Travel agents also offer one-stop inclusive packages, combining air travel with hotel and other ground arrangements at bargain prices.

Read your contract carefully before signing. Most travel agents recommend insurance in case you are forced to cancel your trip because of illness or accident. This is often available as part of a general travel insurance policy.

BY ROAD AND SEA

Car ferries operate daily all the year round from Barcelona and Valencia to Mallorca (an 8-hour, overnight trip); extra boats are put on in the high season, as well as direct links with Menorca, and connections with Algiers. Sailings to Menorca from Barcelona or Palma are much less frequent. In high season, all these services are busy and you should reserve well ahead. If you are coming from Britain or Ireland, the same applies to ferry services linking them to mainland Europe. As well as the many cross-Channel routes, there is a long-distance ferry service from Plymouth to Santander in northern Spain (a 24-hour trip), though that still leaves the drive to Barcelona—some 565 kilometres or 350 miles.

If you are considering taking your car simply because you want one to use on Mallorca or Menorca, remember that renting one there could be more economical (see CAR HIRE).

BY RAIL

Good, though crowded, trains link Spain with the rest of Europe. Seat and sleeper reservations are compulsory on most Spanish trains. With the exception of the *Barcelona-Talgo* and *Euro-City* expresses which have adjustable axles, passengers have to change trains at the French frontier, as Spanish tracks are of a wider gauge. Paris/Barcelona by *Talgo* takes nearly 12 hours, Geneva/Barcelona, 11 hours. Having arrived in Barcelona by train, you can continue to Mallorca or Menorca by sea or by air.

Both *Inter-Rail* and *Rail Europ Senior* cards are valid in Spain, as is the *Eurailpass* for non-European residents (buy before arriving in Europe). For full information, contact the Spanish national railways: RENFE, General Agency for Europe, 1–3 av. Marceau, 75115 Paris.

When to Go

Sun-seekers hit the beaches from May to October and the sea is pleasantly warm for swimming from June or July to October. July and August can be oven-hot as well as very crowded. But Mallorca enjoys a mild winter too, making a tempting break for visitors from northern Europe. It can be chilly and wet at times, of course, but a wall of mountains along the north-west coast protects the rest of the island from the worst of the winter weather. The tourist season has been getting longer: March and April bring a rush of cyclists, soon followed by walkers and bird-watchers.

Menorca lacks the protection of a mountain range, and can be swept by cold winds in winter and early spring. The holiday season there runs from early May to the end of October, with few hotels open the rest of the year.

The average daily temperatures and sunshine figures below apply to Palma. They will help you decide what to take in the way of clothing.

		J	F	M	A	M	J	J	A	S	O	N	D
Maximum	°F	57	59	62	66	71	79	84	84	80	73	65	59
	°C	14	15	17	19	22	26	29	29	27	23	18	15
Minimum	°F	43	44	46	51	55	62	67	68	65	57	50	46
	°C	6	6	8	10	13	17	20	20	18	14	10	8
Days of sunshine		15	14	16	19	20	22	28	26	20	16	14	14

All figures are approximate monthly averages.

Planning Your Budget

To give you an idea of what to expect, here are some average prices in Spanish pesetas. However, they must be regarded as approximate, as inflation pushes costs relentlessly higher. Rates of exchange fluctuate, so check the latest figures for your currency. Prices quoted may be subject to a VAT/sales tax (IVA) of either 6% or 12%.

Airport transfer. Mallorca: bus to Palma 130 ptas., taxi about 700 ptas. Menorca: no airport bus, taxi to Mahón centre about 800 ptas.

Babysitters. 500–800 ptas./hour.

Bicycle and motorscooter hire. Bicycle per day 750 ptas., moped per day 2,000 ptas., scooter per day about 2,500 ptas.

Car hire (unlimited mileage, insurance included). *Seat Marbella* 2,500 ptas./day, 17,000 ptas./week; *Ford Escort* 3,000 ptas./day, 20,000 ptas./week. Add 12% tax. (Note: rates are highly seasonal, and can be much lower if car hire is paid for in advance through travel agents/companies.)

Cigarettes. Spanish brands 60–125 ptas./packet of 20, foreign brands 150–200 ptas./packet of 20.

Entertainment. Bullfight 800 ptas. and up, cinema 450 ptas. and up, nightclub/flamenco/cabaret show 2,000 ptas. and up, disco (admission and first drink) about 1,000 ptas. (some free entry).

Hairdressers. *Woman's* haircut 2,500 ptas., shampoo and set or blow-dry 2,000 ptas.; *man's* haircut 1,500 ptas.

Hotels (double room with bath). ***** 18,000–22,000 ptas., **** 8,000–14,000 ptas., *** 4,000–9,000 ptas., ** 2,500–5,000 ptas., * 2,000–3,500 ptas.

Meals and drinks. Continental breakfast 250–400 ptas., *plato del día* from 600 ptas., *menú del día* from 750 ptas., lunch/dinner in good restaurant 2,000 ptas. and up, beer (small bottle or glass) 100 ptas., coffee 85 ptas., Spanish brandy 200 ptas., soft drinks 125 ptas. and up, bottle of house wine 400 ptas., wines from list 800 ptas. and up.

Shopping bag. Loaf of bread 55–200 ptas., 200g of butter 250 ptas., 6 eggs 120 ptas., beefsteak (500g) 750 ptas., 250g of coffee 225 ptas., 100g of instant coffee 300 ptas., fruit juice (1 litre) 150 ptas., bottle of wine 150 ptas. and up.

Sports. *Golf* green fees 3,000–5,000 ptas. per day, *tennis* court fee 1,000 ptas./hour, *horseback-riding* from 1,500 ptas./hour, *water-skiing* about 1,600 ptas. per round, 2,500 ptas./hour with lesson, *windsurfer* hire about 1,200 ptas./hour (negotiate day rates).

An A-Z Summary of Practical Information and Facts

Listed after some entries is the appropriate Spanish translation, usually in the singular, plus a number of phrases that may come in handy during your stay. You will soon discover, however, that the local dialects of Catalan, called *Mallorquí / Menorquí*, are widely used, including most place names on signs. In that respect this book follows the local usage as far as possible, even if it is not always consistent. A short list of words and phrases in dialect appears on pages 116 and 117.

ACCOMMODATION. Prices are not government-controlled but they must be posted at reception desks and in rooms. Off-season, you may be able to negotiate lower rates, but note that most resort hotels close for the winter, reducing your choice. In the height of summer, they may be filled by the clients of package tour operators who have reserved the accommodation in advance (see also WHEN TO GO, p.103).

    Accommodation ranges across a broad spectrum. You can find a room in a *pensión* (boarding house), *hostal* (modest hotel), resort hotel with sports and entertainment facilities or *de luxe* palace in city or countryside. Breakfast may be included in the room rate: ask. On arrival, a guest normally signs a card which should state the hotel category, room number and room rate as well as the guest's name, passport number, etc. In practice, reception clerks often put these details in later with the aid of the guest's passport, which they keep for a day or so.

    Hotels are officially graded by stars, one to five, according to their facilities. *Hostales* are graded from one to three stars. The grading is posted at the front door.

    Grades are not always a reflection of quality: some one-star places can be superior to others with three. Ancient, sagging beds, for example, are unfortunately common in all grades of accommodation. (Ask for a board to be put under the mattress, or put it on the floor!)

    Increasingly popular in Mediterranean tourism are package arrangements including accommodation in furnished apartments or villas. These are usually part of a complex with joint amenities, such as a swimming pool, gardens or sports facilities, depending on the price. The tour companies' brochures should give a full and accurate description.

A

A   **Youth Hostels** *(albergue de juventud):* There are youth hostels at Ca'n Pastilla (Platja de Palma) and Alcúdia. They are likely to be full in summer.

I'd like a double/single room.	**Quisiera una habitación doble/sencilla.**
with/without bath/shower	**con/sin baño/ducha**
What's the rate per night?	**¿Cuál es el precio por noche?**

AIRPORTS *(aeropuerto)*

Mallorca. Son Sant Joan Airport, Palma de Mallorca (PMI), has two terminals: Terminal A for scheduled flights and some charters, Terminal B for charter flights only. Free luggage trolleys are available and porters are also on hand. A tourist information office, hotel-reservation, car-hire and currency-exchange counters, post office, restaurant, bar, hairdresser, left luggage depot, souvenir and duty-free shops (international departures only) are at your disposal. Taxis and regular buses link the airport with Palma, a 15-minute trip. Official taxi fares to all parts of the island are posted by the airport exit doors. The bus service operates to Plaça de Espanya (the terminal is near Palma's two railway stations) every half-hour from early morning to midnight. Tour-company representatives and hotel coaches meet charter-flight passengers.

Menorca. Mahón (Maó) Airport (MAH) is only 5 kilometres (3 miles), a few minutes' taxi ride, from the city. There are no regular buses. The airport's international traffic is restricted to the summer months from May to October, and many of its facilities (tourist information, duty-free shop) open only during that period. Car-hire desks, café and bar operate year-round.

B   **BICYCLE and MOTORSCOOTER HIRE** *(bicicletas/escúteres de alquiler).* A practical and enjoyable way to see the islands is to hire a bicycle by the hour or day. Mopeds and motorscooters are also available in most resorts, but you'll need a licence exclusively for them. Prices vary widely, so shop around. Remember that wearing crash-helmets is compulsory when riding a motorcycle, whatever the engine capacity, though you'd never guess it from seeing the locals.

I'd like to hire a bicycle.	**Quisiera alquilar una bicicleta.**
What's the charge per day/week?	**¿Cuánto cobran por día/ semana?**

CAMPING *(camping)*. Organized campsites are almost non-existent: those near Ca'n Picafort and San Pedro on Mallorca, and near Son Bou and Cala Galdana on Menorca, are exceptions. You may be able to camp on private land, but be sure to ask permission of the owner first.

May we camp here?	**¿Podemos acampar aquí?**
We have a tent.	**Tenemos una tienda de camping.**

CAR HIRE *(coches de alquiler)*. There are car-hire firms in most resorts, main towns and at the airports. Ask for special seasonal rates and discounts and find out what insurance cover is included. A value-added tax (IVA) of 12% is added to the total charge, but will have been included if you have pre-paid the car hire before arrival (normally the way to obtain the lowest rates). Third-party insurance is included, but full collision coverage is advisable as well. Unlimited free mileage is always included in the Balearics. General conditions may include a refundable deposit, but holders of major credit cards are usually exempt.

You should be over 21, and have had your full licence at least 6 months. You should also have an International Driving Permit, but the hire companies in practice accept your ordinary national licence. So, probably, will the police if you are stopped by them, though they might insist on an official Spanish translation.

Most sizes of car are available, including 4-wheel drives and convertibles, but the vast majority are small economy models. They're well suited to the narrow rural roads and mountain hairpin bends.

I'd like to rent a car (tomorrow).	**Quisiera alquilar un coche (para mañana).**
for one day/a week	**por un día/una semana**
Please include full insurance cover.	**Haga el favor de incluir el seguro a todo riesgo.**

CIGARETTES, CIGARS, TOBACCO *(cigarrillos, puros, tabaco)*. Spanish cigarettes can be made of strong, black tobacco *(negro)* or light tobacco *(rubio)*. Foreign brands are two or three times as expensive as the domestic product. Spanish cigars are cheap but can be rough, those from the Canary Islands are better than most. Cuban cigars are readily available. Most foreigners find Spanish pipe tobacco rather harsh, but imported brands are much more expensive. Dedicated pipe-smokers will take their own supply.

107

C **COMMUNICATIONS.** Post offices *(correos)* are for mail and telegrams: you can't usually telephone from them.

Post office hours: 9 a.m. to 2 p.m. Monday to Friday; 9 a.m. to 1 p.m. Saturday. The main post offices in Palma and Mahón also open from 4 to 6 p.m. (Mon-Fri) for stamps.

Stamps *(sello)* can also be bought at some shops which sell postcards and cigarettes.

Mail: If you don't know in advance where you'll be staying, you can have your mail addressed to the *Lista de Correos* (poste restante or general delivery) in the nearest town. Take your passport to the post office as identification when you want to collect any letters. There may be a small charge.

Mailboxes are bright yellow.

Telegrams *(telegrama):* The main telegraph offices are at the main post offices: in Palma at Constitució 6, tel. 72 20 00; in Mahón at Bonaire 15, tel. 36 38 95. Telegrams are expensive, and remember that there is no telegram delivery in the U.K. It will usually be quicker, cheaper and more convenient to telephone.

Telephone *(teléfono):* The telephone office is independent of the post office. It is identified by a blue and white sign. You can make direct-dial local and international calls from coin-operated telephone booths in the the street. Instructions for use are given in several languages in the booths, which are widely distributed throughout the islands. Calls can also be made from hotels, usually with a surcharge.

For international calls, have a supply of coins (25, 50 or 100 ptas.; don't use 5 ptas. coins which may break the connection). Pick up the receiver, wait for the dialling tone, dial 07, wait for a further tone and then dial the country code, area code (without initial 0) and number. The coins will drop in as needed from the slot provided. Some country codes:

Australia	(07) 61	New Zealand	(07) 64
Canada	(07) 1	U.K.	(07) 44
Eire	(07) 353	U.S.A.	(07) 1

Dial the operator (9398) if you wish to make a person-to-person *(persona a persona)* call or to reverse the charges/make a collect call *(cobro revertido),* for which you have to make a 700 ptas. deposit—refunded if the call is accepted.

Can you get me this number in...?	**¿Puede comunicarme con este número en...?**
Have you received any mail for...?	**¿Ha recibido correo para...?**

A stamp for this letter/postcard please.	**Por favor, un sello para esta carta/tarjeta postal.**
express (special delivery)	**urgente**
airmail	**vía aérea**
registered	**certificado**
I would like to send a telegram to...	**Quisiera mandar un telegrama a...**

COMPLAINTS. By law, all hotels, restaurants and campsites must have official complaint forms *(Hoja Oficial de Reclamación/Full Oficial de Reclamació)* and produce them on demand. The original of this document should be sent to the regional office of the Ministry of Tourism, one copy remains with the establishment complained against and you keep the third sheet. Merely asking for a complaint form is often enough to resolve most matters since tourism authorities take a serious view of complaints and your hosts want to keep both their reputation and licence.

Legislation has been introduced that greatly strengthens the consumer's hand. Public information offices are being set up, inspections carried out and inaccurate information made punishable by law. You might be referred to the consumer protection office (Dirección General de Consumo, via Roma 18, Palma). For a tourist's needs, however, the tourist office, or in really serious cases, the police, would be able to handle the situation or at least advise where to go. In Palma, the police can call upon interpreters in the main foreign languages spoken by visitors.

CONSULATES *(consulado)*

Canada:	For minor matters contact the British consulate, Palma (or Honorary Vice-Consul, Menorca). Other cases: Consulate General, Edif. Goya, Calle Núñez de Balboa 35, 28001 Madrid; tel. 431 43 00
Eire:	(Honorary Consul): Sant Miquel 68 (8th fl.), Palma; tel. 71 92 44
U.K.:	(also for Commonwealth citizens): Plaça Major 3-D, Palma; tel. 71 24 45 (Honorary Vice-Consul, Menorca): Carrer Torret 28, Sant Lluis; tel. 36 64 39
U.S.A.:	(consular agency): Avda. del Rei Jaume III 26, Palma; tel. 72 26 60

Where's the British/American consulate?	**¿Dónde está el consulado británico/americano?**

C CONVERSION CHARTS. For fluid and distance measures, see p.113. Spain uses the metric system.

Temperature

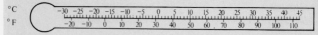

Length

Weight

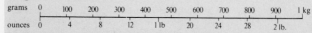

CRIME and THEFT.
Spain's crime rate has caught up with that of other European countries and the Balearics have not been immune. Be on your guard against purse-snatchers and pickpockets, especially in busy places, markets, fiestas, sports events and Palma streets (particularly the area of Plaça Major, which should be given a wide berth at night).

The rules are the ones you might follow almost anywhere. Don't leave valuables unattended and avoid taking them to the beach. Make use of hotel safe-boxes. Don't carry large sums of money or expensive jewellery. Lock cars and never leave cases, bags, cameras, etc., on view.

In Palma or Manacor, report thefts and break-ins to the Policía Nacional, elsewhere to the Guardia Civil.

I want to report a theft.	**Quiero denunciar un robo.**
My handbag/ticket/wallet/ passport has been stolen.	**Me han robado el bolso/ el billete/la cartera/el pasaporte.**

CUSTOMS (aduana) and ENTRY REGULATIONS.
Most visitors require only a valid passport to enter Spain (and for U.K. citizens, resident in the U.K., the simpler British Visitor's Passport is also acceptable). Visitors from South Africa, however, must have visas, and those from Australia may only stay for one month and make no more than two entries in that time, unless they have a visa. New Zealanders are

permitted one month's stay and only one entry per year without a visa. Most visitors are allowed to stay for 90 days (U.S. citizens 180 days). If in doubt, and because regulations are liable to change, check with your travel agent before departure.

Into:	Cigarettes		Cigars		Tobacco	Spirits		Wine
Spain 1)	300	or	75	or	400 g.	1.5 l.	and	5 l.
2)	200	or	50	or	250 g.	1 l.	and	2 l.
Australia	200	or	250 g.	or	250 g.	1 l.	or	1 l.
Canada	200	and	50	and	900 g.	1.1 l.	or	1.1 l.
Eire*	200	or	50	or	250 g.	1 l.	and	2 l.
Eire†	300	or	75	or	400 g.	1.5 l.	and	5 l.
N. Zealand	200	or	50	or	250 g.	1.1 l.	and	4.5 l.
S. Africa	400	and	50	and	250 g.	1 l.	and	2 l.
U.K.*	200	or	50	or	250 g.	1 l.	and	2 l.
U.K.†	300	or	75	or	400 g.	1.5 l.	and	5 l.
U.S.A.	200	and	100	and	3)	1 l.	or	1 l.

1) Visitors arriving from EEC countries, goods on which duty has been paid.
2) Visitors arriving from other countries, and from EEC countries, duty-free goods.
3) A reasonable quantity.
* Allowance for duty-free goods.
† Allowance for goods on which duty has been paid.

Currency restrictions. There are no limits on the amount of money, Spanish or foreign, that you may import. Departing, you should declare amounts beyond the equivalent of 500,000 ptas. It would be wise, therefore, to declare such amounts on entry if you plan to carry them out again.

DRIVING IN SPAIN. To take your car into Spain, you should have:

• your driving licence, and an International Driving Permit (not obligatory for citizens of most Western European countries—ask your automobile association—but recommended in case of difficulties as it carries a text in Spanish) or a legalized and certified translation of your driving licence

• car registration papers

• Green Card (an extension to your regular insurance policy, making it valid for foreign countries)

• nationality sticker on the back of the vehicle.

D *Also strongly recommended:* A bail bond, obtainable from your insurance company or automobile association. If you were to injure somebody in Spain, you could be imprisoned while the accident is under investigation. This bond will bail you out.

When driving, be sure to carry all the required papers (or photocopies), including car hire documents.

Driving conditions on Mallorca and Menorca: The rules are the same as in mainland Spain: drive on the right, overtake (pass) on the left, yield right of way to vehicles coming from the right (unless your road is marked as having priority). Seat belt use is compulsory and may be enforced by fines. Although in towns the local drivers still seem unconvinced, they buckle up on the open road.

Main roads are well-surfaced and are constantly being improved. Mallorca has a few short but increasing stretches of motorway. Secondary roads on Mallorca are narrow but good; on Menorca they can be very narrow, rough and unsignposted. Minor "roads" no better than stony cart-tracks abound, especially on Menorca, where you'll find yourself taking them if you go exploring.

Quaint attractions—horse-drawn carts and farm animals—can be perils on the road. When passing through villages, beware of children darting out of doorways and older folk strolling in the middle of the road, especially after dark.

Traffic police: The roads are patrolled by the Traffic Civil Guard (*Guardia Civil de Tráfico*) in pairs on powerful black motorcycles. Courteous and helpful, they are also tough on lawbreakers. Fines are payable on the spot. You might be stopped for:
• speeding
• travelling too close to the car in front
• overtaking (passing) without using your direction indicators
• travelling at night with a burned-out light (Spanish law requires you to carry a full set of spare bulbs at all times)
• failing to come to a complete halt at a stop sign

Speed limits: 120 kph (75 mph) on motorways, 100 kph (62 mph) on broad main roads (two lanes each way), 90 kph (56 mph) on other main roads, 60 kph (37 mph), or as marked, in built-up areas.

Beware of drinking and driving. The permitted blood-alcohol level is low, easily exceeded in a holiday atmosphere, and fines for doing so are intended to deter.

Parking can be difficult in towns. Foreign and mainland-registered vehicles are not immune from wheel-clamping and towing away if they park illegally or overstay time limits.

Fuel and oil: Service stations are plentiful on Mallorca but not Menorca. Petrol (gasoline) comes in 92 (normal), 95 (lead-free) and 97 (super) grades, but not all at every station. Diesel fuel is widely available.

Fluid measures

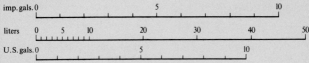

Distance

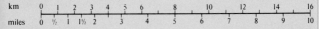

Breakdowns: Balearic garages are as efficient as any, and the mechanics can be ingenious, but repairs may take time in busy tourist areas. Spare parts are readily available for Spanish-built cars and many other popular models. For less common makes, they may have to be imported. Kits of basic spare parts are obtainable from some automobile associations (for refund on return home if not used). Make sure your car is in top shape before you leave home.

Road signs: Most signs are the standard pictographs used throughout Europe. However, you may encounter the following written signs, in Spanish or amended into *Mallorquí* or *Menorquí*.

¡Alto!	Stop!
Apague las luces	Switch off lights
Aparcamiento	Parking
Autopista	Motorway
Calzada deteriorada	Bad road
Calzada estrecha	Narrow road
Ceda el paso	Give way (yield)
Cruce peligroso	Dangerous crossroads
Cuidado	Caution
Curva peligrosa	Dangerous bend
Desprendimientos	Landslides
Despacio	Slow
Desviación	Diversion
Encienda las luces	Switch on lights
Escuela	School
Grúa	Tow-away area

D	Peligro	Danger
	Prohibido adelantar	No overtaking (passing)
	Prohibido aparcar	No parking
	Puesto de socorro	First-aid post
	Recuerde	Restriction continues
	Salida (de camiones)	(Lorry/truck) exit

(International) Driving Permit	**Carné de conducir (internacional)**
Car registration papers	**Permiso de circulación**
Green Card	**Carta verde**
Are we on the right road for...?	**¿Es ésta la carretera hacia...?**
Full tank, please.	**Llene el depósito, por favor.**
normal	**normal**
super	**super**
lead-free	**sin plomo**
Please check the oil/tyres/battery.	**Por favor, controle el aceite/los neumáticos/la batería.**
Can I park here?	**¿Puedo aparcar aquí?**
My car has broken down.	**Mi coche se ha estropeado.**
There's been an accident.	**Ha habido un accidente.**

DRUGS. At one time in the 1980s, the possession of small amounts of soft drugs for personal use was legalized. Now the pendulum has swung back, and possession and sale of drugs are again criminal offences in Spain.

E **ELECTRIC CURRENT** *(corriente eléctrica)* of 220 volts is almost standard, but older installations of 125 volts, although becoming rare in tourist facilities, may still be found, sometimes alongside the 220-volt system. Check before plugging in. If the voltage is 125, American appliances will operate. If it is 220, you will need a transformer to operate them.

What's the voltage?	**¿Cuál es el voltaje?**
an adaptor/a battery	**un adaptador/una pila**

EMERGENCIES. (See also CONSULATES, MEDICAL CARE, POLICE.) If you are not staying in a hotel, telephone or visit the local Municipal Police or the Guardia Civil. Try to take a Spanish speaker with you. Here are a few important telephone numbers:

	MALLORCA	MENORCA
Police	091	091
First aid *(casa de socorro)*	72 21 79 (Palma)	36 12 21 (Mahón)
Fire brigade *(bomberos)*	080 (Palma)	36 39 61 (Mahón)

(Check front of phone book for other places.)

Careful!	¡Cuidado!	Police!	¡Policía!
Fire!	¡Fuego!	Stop!	¡Deténgase!
Help!	¡Socorro!	Stop thief!	¡Al ladrón!

FIRE *(incendio).* Forest fires are a menace on Mallorca, particularly in the mountainous north where the only way to fight them may be by aerial bombardment. On Menorca, too, undergrowth may be tinder-dry. So be careful where you throw matches and cigarette ends. Any campfires must be doused with water and covered with earth before you move on. In some areas, signs indicate a complete ban on fires.

GUIDES and INTERPRETERS *(guía, intérprete).* On Mallorca, apply to the Grupo Sindical de Informadores Turísticos, Miquel Marqués 13, Palma (near the railway and bus terminals); tel. 46 09 30.

On Menorca, a list is available at the Tourist Information Office, Plaça Esplanada 40, Mahón); tel. 36 08 79.

We'd like an English-speaking guide.	Queremos un guía que hable inglés.
I need an English interpreter.	Necesito un intérprete de inglés.

HAIRDRESSERS *(peluquería)* **and BARBERS** *(barbería).* Many larger hotels have their own salons, and the standard is generally good. Prices vary widely. Most include a service charge in their prices but it is still the custom to give a tip of about 10%.

haircut	corte
shampoo and set	lavado y marcado
blow-dry	modelado
permanent wave	permanente

HOURS. Schedules revolve around the siesta, a great Spanish custom aimed at keeping people out of the hottest sun. To accommodate the midday pause, most shops and offices open from 9 a.m. to 1 or 2 p.m. and

H again from 4 or 5 p.m. until 8 p.m. or later. Big supermarkets may stay open throughout the day.

Restaurants serve lunch from 1 to 3.30 p.m. In the evenings their timing depends on the kind of customers they expect. Locals probably want to eat between 8.30 and 11 p.m. (rather earlier than on the mainland); places catering for foreigners may function from 7 p.m.

L **LANGUAGE.** The islands are bilingual (at least). The national language, Castilian Spanish, is understood everywhere. But in addition, *Mallorquí* is spoken in Mallorca and *Menorquí* in Menorca. These are dialects of Catalan, the language of eastern Spain and parts of the French Pyrenees.

Many islanders speak Castilian with a marked but clear accent, which some foreigners, struggling along with school Spanish, may find easier to follow than mainland pronunciation.

English is widely understood in resort areas and by people used to dealing with visitors. So to a lesser extent are German and French.

	MALLORQUÍ/MENORQUÍ	CASTILIAN
Welcome	*Benvinguts*	*Bienvenido*
Good morning	*Bon dia*	*Buenos días*
Good afternoon/evening	*Bona tarda*	*Buenas tardes*
Good night	*Bon nit*	*Buenas noches*
Please	*Si us plau*	*Por favor*
Thank you	*Graciès*	*Gracias*
Goodbye	*Adéu*	*Adiós*

(See also MAPS AND PLACE NAMES.)

Everywhere you'll hear an indispensable, all-purpose Spanish expression. Said with a shrug, it can mean anything from "you're welcome" to "who cares?". The phrase is: *es igual* ("it's the same").

The Berlitz phrase book, SPANISH FOR TRAVELLERS, covers most situations you're likely to encounter in your travels through the islands. And the Berlitz Spanish-English/English-Spanish pocket dictionary contains a 12,500-word glossary of each language, plus a menu-reader supplement.

LAUNDRY *(lavandería)* **and DRY-CLEANING** *(tintorería)*. Most hotels will handle laundry and dry-cleaning but they'll usually charge more than an independent establishment. Major resorts have self-service launderettes and the best-equipped villas and apartments have washing

116 machines.

Where's the nearest laundry/dry-cleaners?	**¿Dónde está la lavandería/ tintorería más cercana?**
When will it be ready?	**¿Cuándo estará listo?**
I must have this for tomorrow morning.	**Lo necesito para mañana por la mañana.**

LOST PROPERTY. The first thing to do when you discover you've lost something is, obviously, to retrace your steps. If nothing comes to light, report the loss to the Municipal Police or Guardia Civil. You will need a copy of the report if you are going to make a claim on an insurance policy.

| I've lost my wallet/handbag/ passport. | **He perdido mi cartera/bolso/ pasaporte.** |

MAPS and PLACE NAMES. With the resurgence of the islands' own dialects, places and streets previously named in Castilian Spanish on signs and maps are now usually given in local forms. Both may be used interchangeably, causing visitors some confusion, compounded by some politically motivated renaming of streets and squares and by the spray-painting of signs by linguistic nationalists. Enjoy the fun by spotting the biggest changes (like Es Migjorn Gran, *Menorquí* for San Cristóbal).

MALLORQUÍ/MENORQUÍ	CASTILIAN	ENGLISH
Aeroport	**Aeropuerto**	Airport
Avinguda	**Avenida**	Avenue
Camí	**Camino**	Road
Carrer	**Calle**	Street
Castell	**Castillo**	Castle
Centre	**Centro**	Centre
Cova	**Cueva**	Cave
Església	**Iglesia**	Church
Mercat	**Mercado**	Market
Palau	**Palacio**	Palace
Passaig	**Pasaje**	Passageway
Passeig	**Paseo**	Boulevard
Plaça	**Plaza**	Square
Platja	**Playa**	Beach
Poble	**Pueblo**	Small town

Ca'n, which appears in so many place names, originally meant "house of", and *Son,* "estate or farm". *Bini,* derived from Arabic, signified "the sons of" (i.e. family). *Cala* means "cove".

Don't hesitate to ask for local help if you are puzzled and can't find a street you are looking for. People are remarkably helpful. The maps in

117

M this guide were prepared by Falk-Verlag, who also publish a map of Mallorca and Menorca.

I'd like a street plan/ a road map.	**Quisiera un plano de la ciudad/ un mapa de carreteras.**

MEDICAL CARE. Standards of hygiene are generally high, and the "usual" intestinal disorder of travellers, if it occurs, is more likely to be due to an excess of sun or alcohol.

It is well worth taking out insurance to cover the risk of illness or accident when on holiday. This is normally available as part of a general travel insurance package.

There are doctors in all towns and their consulting hours are displayed. For less serious matters, first-aid personnel, called *practicantes,* make daily rounds of the larger resort hotels, and some hotels have a nurse on duty. In case of need, enquire at your hotel, or, away from hotels, ask the police or tourist offices for help.

Pharmacies *(farmacia)* are open during normal shopping hours but there is at least one per town open all night, the *farmacia de guardia.* Its location is posted in the windows of all other pharmacies. Pharmacists are highly trained and respected in Spain, and for minor problems you can consult them with confidence before or instead of going to a doctor.

Hospitals
Mallorca: Hospital Son Dureta, Andrea Doria 55, Palma, tel. 28 91 00; Clínica Femenia, C. José Cela 20, Palma, tel. 45 23 23.

Menorca: Hospital Municipal, Cos de Gracia 26, Mahón, tel. 36 12 21.

U.K. citizens with a form E.111 obtained well before departure from the Department of Health can receive free emergency treatment at Social Security and Municipal hospitals in Spain.

Where's the nearest (all-night) pharmacy?	**¿Dónde está la farmacia (de guardia) más cercana?**
I need a doctor/dentist.	**Necesito un médico/dentista.**
I've a pain here.	**Me duele aquí.**
a fever/sunburn	**fiebre/quemadura del sol**
an upset stomach	**molestias de estómago**
headache	**dolor de cabeza**

MEETING AND GREETING. Although their patience must be tried by the annual rush of visitors, the islanders remain open and hospitable, easy to talk to and generous. The tourist trade has taken the Balearics from poverty to the top of the prosperity table among Spanish regions, but attitudes remain down-to-earth. Neither Mallorcans nor Menorcans like to be categorized with Catalans, despite the similar language and heritage. Nor do they like to be lumped together, as each island has its distinct character.

Politeness and simple courtesies still matter. A handshake on greeting and leaving is normal. Always begin any conversation, whether with a friend, shop assistant, taxi-driver or telephone operator, with a *buenos días* (good morning) or *buenas tardes* (good afternoon). *¡Hola!* (Hello!) is a frequent island substitute. Always say *adiós* (goodbye) or *buenas noches* (good night) when leaving. *Por favor* (please) should begin all requests.

How are you?	**¿Cómo está usted?**
Do you speak English?	**¿Habla usted inglés?**
I don't speak Spanish.	**No hablo español.**

MONEY MATTERS

Currency: The monetary unit of Spain is the *peseta* (abbreviated *pta.*). Coins: 1, 2, 5, 10, 25, 50, 100, 200, 500 pesetas. Banknotes: 200, 500 (both being phased out), 1,000, 2,000, 5,000, 10,000 pesetas.

A 5-peseta coin is traditionally called a *duro*, so if someone asks you for 10 duros, he means 50 pesetas.

For currency restrictions, see CUSTOMS AND ENTRY REGULATIONS.

Banking hours: Banks generally open from 8.30 or 9 a.m. to 2.30 p.m. Monday to Friday (1.30 p.m. in summer) and on Saturdays from 9 a.m. to 1 p.m. (not in summer). Hours vary from town to town. Some banks stay open until 4.30 p.m. (Mon-Thurs, mid-September to mid-June).

Credit cards: The major international cards are widely recognized, though smaller businesses tend to prefer cash. Cards linked to Visa/Eurocard/MasterCard are most generally accepted. They are also useful for obtaining cash advances from banks.

Eurocheques: You'll have no problem settling bills with Eurocheques, provided you have the Eurocheque encashment card.

Exchange offices: Many travel agencies and other businesses displaying a *cambio* sign will change foreign currency into pesetas, and stay open outside banking hours. The rate is likely to be a bit less favourable than at the banks. Both banks and exchange offices pay slightly more for traveller's cheques than for cash. Always take your passport when you go to change money.

M **Paying cash:** Although many shops and bars will accept foreign currencies, they will give you a lower rate than the banks. You are better off paying in pesetas.

Traveller's cheques: Hotels, shops, restaurants and travel agencies accept them, and so do banks, where you're likely to get a better rate. (You will need your passport when cashing them). It is a good plan to hold some of your holiday funds in cheques, cashing small amounts at a time and keeping the rest in the hotel safe if possible. Keep a record of the serial numbers separately to facilitate a refund in case of loss or theft.

Where's the nearest bank/ currency exchange office?	**¿Dónde está el banco/la oficina de cambio más cercana?**
I want to change some pounds/ dollars.	**Quiero cambiar libras/ dólares.**
Do you accept traveller's cheques?	**¿Aceptan cheques de viaje?**
Can I pay with this credit card?	**¿Puedo pagar con esta tarjeta de crédito?**
How much is that?	**¿Cuánto es?**

MOSQUITOES. There are rarely more than a few mosquitoes at any time, but they survive the year round, and just one can ruin a night's sleep. Few hotels in the islands have mosquito-proof windows, though you'll often want to leave them open. Bring your own anti-mosquito devices, whether nets, buzzers, sprays, lotions or incense-type coils that burn all night. Some are available locally too, and you can usually borrow a spray from hotel reception desks.

N **NEWSPAPERS and MAGAZINES** (*periódico; revista*). In main tourist areas most European, including British, newspapers are sold on the day of publication. So are the Paris-based *The International Herald Tribune* and European edition of *The Wall Street Journal*. Principal European and American magazines are available.

The *Mallorca—Daily Bulletin* ("Daily Bee") is a newspaper published six days a week in Palma for English-speaking residents and visitors. It concentrates on national and international news with the accent on Britain and the Balearics, plus a leavening of gossip and "weird" stories ("Snake shoots hunter"). A number of other magazines published locally or in mainland Spain deal with subjects interesting to tourists or residents. On Menorca, you can find a monthly English-language paper called *Roqueta*.

Have you any English-language newspapers/magazines?	**¿Tienen periódicos/revistas en inglés?**

POLICE *(policía).* There are three police forces in Spain: the *Policía Municipal,* who are attached to the local town hall, the *Cuerpo Nacional de Policía,* a national anti-crime unit, and the *Guardia Civil,* the national police force patrolling town and country, including the roads.

If you need police assistance, you can call on any one of the three. Spanish police are efficient, strict and particularly courteous to foreign visitors.

Where's the nearest police station?	**¿Dónde está la comisaría más cercana?**

PUBLIC HOLIDAYS *(fiesta)*

January 1	*Año Nuevo*	New Year's Day
January 6	*Epifanía*	Epiphany
January 20	*San Sebastián*	St. Sebastian's Day
March 19	*San José*	St. Joseph's Day
May 1	*Día del Trabajo*	Labour Day
July 25	*Santiago Apóstol*	St. James's Day
August 15	*Asunción*	Assumption
October 12	*Día de la Hispanidad*	Discovery of America Day (Columbus Day)
November 1	*Todos los Santos*	All Saints' Day
December 6	*Día de la Constitución Española*	Constitution Day
December 25	*Navidad*	Christmas Day
December 26	*La Fiesta Navidad*	Christmas Holiday
Movable dates:	*Jueves Santo*	Maundy Thursday
	Viernes Santo	Good Friday
	Lunes de Pascua	Easter Monday (Balearics)
	Corpus Christi	Corpus Christi
	Inmaculada Concepción	Immaculate Conception (normally December 8)

RADIO and TV *(radio, televisión).* A short-wave set of reasonable quality will pick up all European capitals. Reception of Britain's BBC World Service is usually good to excellent. Especially in winter and in the early morning or evening, a good set will receive the BBC long-wave and even medium-wave domestic programmes.

The Voice of America usually comes through loud and clear, though in the Balearics it is not received 24 hours a day.

R   Most hotels and bars have television, usually tuned to sports (international or local), and broadcasting in Castilian, Catalan (from Barcelona) and *Mallorquí*. Satellite dishes are sprouting, and feeding multiple channels (German, French, Sky, BBC, CNN, Super, etc.) to many hotels and private homes.

T   **TIME DIFFERENCES.** The Balearics keep the same time as mainland Spain. This chart shows the difference between Spain and some selected cities.

Los Angeles	Chicago	New York	London	**Mallorca**
3 a.m.	5 a.m.	6 a.m.	11 a.m.	**noon**

As in the U.K., Eire, the U.S. and Canada, clocks in Spain are turned ahead one hour in spring and back one hour in autumn.

What time is it?   **¿Qué hora es?**

TIPPING. Since a service charge is normally included in hotel and restaurant bills, tipping is not obligatory. However, it's normal to leave a small coin (up to 5% of the bill) after service at a bar counter, and 5–10% on restaurant bills. If you pay by credit card, waiters have a habit of leaving the bottom line open for you to include a tip. Whether you do so or not, fill in the final total. Further rough guidelines:

Airport or station porter	300 ptas.
Hotel porter, per bag	200 ptas.
Maid, for extra services	100–200 ptas.
Lavatory attendant	25–50 ptas.
Waiter	10% (optional)
Taxi driver	10% (optional)
Hairdresser/Barber	10%
Tourist guide	10%
Usher	25–50 ptas.

TOILETS. There are many expressions for "toilets" in Spanish: *aseos, servicios, W.C., water* and *retretes*. The first two terms are the more
122   common. Toilet doors are distinguished by a "C" for *Caballeros*

(gentlemen), or by an "S" for *Señoras* (ladies), or by a variety of pictographs. Public toilets exist in some large towns, rarely elsewhere. But just about every bar and restaurant has one available for public use. It's considered polite to buy a coffee or drink if you drop in specifically to use the conveniences.

Where are the toilets?   **¿Dónde están los servicios?**

TOURIST INFORMATION OFFICES (*oficina de turismo*). Spanish National Tourist Offices are maintained in many countries throughout the world:

Australia: International House, Suite 44, 104 Bathurst St., P.O.Box A-675, 2000 Sydney NSW; tel. (02) 264 79 66

Canada: 60 Bloor St. West, Suite 201, Toronto, Ontario M5W 3B8; tel. (416) 961-31 31

U.K: 57–58 St. James's St., London SW1A 1LD; tel. (071) 499-0901

U.S.A: Water Tower Place, Suite 915 East, 845 North Michigan Ave., Chicago, IL 60611; tel. (312) 944-0216/230-9025

The Galleria, Suite 4800, 5085 Westheimer Rd., Houston, TX 77056; tel. (713) 840-7411/13

8383 Wilshire Blvd., Suite 960, 90211 Beverly Hills, CA 90211; tel. (213) 658-7188/93

665 5th Ave., New York, NY 10022; tel. (212) 759-8822

Major resorts on Mallorca have their own tourist information offices. In Palma: Oficina de Información Turística, Avinguda del Rei Jaume III 10; tel. 71 22 16. Fomento del Turismo, Carrer de Constitució 1; tel. 72 53 96. Oficina de Información Turística, Palma Airport; tel. 26 08 03.
  On Menorca: Oficina de Información Turística, Plaça Esplanada, Mahón; tel. 36 37 90.

Where is the tourist office?   **¿Dónde está la oficina de turismo?**

TRANSPORT

Buses: Mallorca is well served by bus lines. Destinations are usually clearly marked on the front of the bus. Additional buses operate between Palma and the principal beaches during the summer season. Each town

T has its main bus stop or terminal. In Palma, most services start from Plaça de Espanya, Plaça Sant Antoní or Plaça de la Reina.

Menorca's bus system is much more limited, but services run between the main towns. In Mahón most start from Plaça Esplanada or nearby Avinguda J. M. Quadrado.

A return (round-trip) bus ticket is always cheaper than an advertised travel-agency tour. For information on timetables and fares, ask at a bus station *(estación de autobuses),* or at any tourist information office.

Taxis: Spanish taxis compare very favourably with those in other countries. It's a good idea to check the fare before you get in: rates are fixed and published, and rate cards in several languages are carried in the taxi. If you take a long trip, for example between two villages, you may be charged a two-way fare whether you return or not.

Trains *(tren):* Mallorca has two narrow-gauge lines, starting from neighbouring stations on Plaça de Espanya, Palma. One goes to Inca, making numerous trips each day. The more picturesque line, both for scenery and vintage rolling stock, links Palma and Sóller (see p. 43), and makes five runs in each direction every day (six on Sundays). There's a tourist special at 10.40 a.m. from Palma, making an extra stop in the mountains above Sóller.

When's the next bus/train to...?	**¿Cuándo sale el próximo autobús/tren para...?**
A ticket to...	**Un billete para...**
single (one-way)	**ida**
return (round-trip)	**ida y vuelta**
What's the fare to...?	**¿Cuánto es la tarifa a ...?**
first/second class	**primera/segunda clase**
Would you tell me when to get off?	**¿Podría indicarme cuándo tengo que bajar?**
I'd like to make seat reservations.	**Quiero reservar asientos.**
Where can I get a taxi?	**¿Dónde puedo coger un taxi?**

W **WATER.** Tap water in the Balearics is safe to drink, but can taste very "flat", strange and sometimes salty. It does not enhance mixed drinks. Most local people drink bottled water, *agua con gas* (carbonated) or *sin gas* (still), and you will probably prefer to do the same. It is good, clean and not expensive.

a bottle of mineral water	**una botella de agua mineral**
Is this drinking water?	**¿El agua es potable?**

SOME USEFUL EXPRESSIONS

yes/no	**sí/no**
please/thank you	**por favor/gracias**
excuse me/you're welcome	**perdone/de nada**
where/when/how	**dónde/cuándo/cómo**
how long/how far	**cuánto tiempo/a qué distancia**
yesterday/today/tomorrow	**ayer/hoy/mañana**
day/week/month/year	**día/semana/mes/año**
left/right	**izquierda/derecha**
up/down	**arriba/abajo**
good/bad	**bueno/malo**
big/small	**grande/pequeño**
cheap/expensive	**barato/caro**
hot/cold	**caliente/frío**
old/new	**viejo/nuevo**
open/closed	**abierto/cerrado**
here/there	**aquí/allí**
free(vacant)/occupied	**libre/ocupado**
early/late	**temprano/tarde**
easy/difficult	**fácil/difícil**
Does anyone here speak English?	**¿Hay alguien aquí que hable inglés?**
What does this mean?	**¿Qué quiere decir esto?**
I don't understand.	**No comprendo.**
Please write it down.	**Escríbamelo, por favor.**
Is there an admission charge?	**¿Se debe pagar la entrada?**
Waiter!/Waitress!	**¡Camarero!/¡Camarera!**
I'd like...	**Quisiera...**
How much is that?	**¿Cuánto es?**
Have you something less expensive?	**¿Tiene algo más barato?**
Just a minute.	**Un momento.**
Help me, please.	**Ayúdeme, por favor.**
Get a doctor, quickly!	**¡Llamen a un médico, rápidamente!**

Index

An asterisk (*) next to a page number indicates a map reference. Where there is more than one set of page references, the one in bold type refers to the main entry. Except for Menorca listings, place names refer to Mallorca. For index to Practical Information, see inside front cover.